THE

FARMERS

DINNER

COOKBOOK

THE FARMERS DINNER COOKBOOK

13-Digit ISBN: 978-1-60433-863-8
10-Digit ISBN: 1-60433-863-6

This book may be ordered by mail from the publisher. Please include $5.99 for postage and handling. Please support your local bookseller first!

Books published by Cider Mill Press Book Publishers are available at special discounts for bulk purchases in the United States by corporations, institutions, and other organizations. For more information, please contact the publisher.

Cider Mill Press Book Publishers
"Where good books are ready for press"
PO Box 454
12 Spring Street
Kennebunkport, Maine 04046
Visit us online!
cidermillpress.com

Typography: Cambria, Hanley Block Display, Hanley Sans, Hanley Script, URW DIN

Printed in China

1 2 3 4 5 6 7 8 9 0

First Edition

THE

FARMERS

DINNER

COOKBOOK

A STORY IN EVERY BITE

OVER 150

Seasonal Recipes

KEITH SARASIN & CHRIS VIAUD

BOOK
PUBLISHERS
KENNEBUNKPORT, MAINE

CONTENTS

INTRODUCTION

DISCOVERING THE MISSING LINK

BY CHRIS VIAUD

AS A KID I always enjoyed helping my mom in the kitchen with basic prep work, such as grinding herbs, spices, and aromatics using a mortar and pestle, or cutting vegetables that would be used for soups and stews. I also spent a lot of time watching cooking shows on television. These were the experiences that made me want to become a chef. And, after four years of studying and learning at Johnson & Wales, my interest became a passion, resulting in a sense of clarity and validation about my career that I carry with me to this day.

Over the years I have worked in restaurants with many different cooking styles and levels of service. I always enjoyed working with high-quality ingredients, but when creating dishes I felt as though I was missing something. I wanted to find purpose and meaning in the food I was presenting. A couple of chefs that I became friends with, including my co-author Keith Sarasin, provided me with a list of local farms. I began reaching out to those farmers, building relationships with them, and finding out what it is that makes their products so special. I had found the missing link—the story.

Farmers, fishermen, and foragers all have stories to tell. As I got to know them, I began to create dishes that reflected these stories. This pursuit, which was enriched as I got to know more and more about my local suppliers, provided me with a whole new way of cooking and thinking about food.

After this discovery, I reached out to Keith because I knew The Farmers Dinner utilized a similar approach while hosting multiple-course meals at beautiful local farms. Since joining The Farmers Dinner, I have toured the fields with farmers, listened to their stories of triumph and defeat, and learned more about growing cycles and what items they have a hard time selling.

The majority of the time our walks through the fields dictate how Keith and I plan our menus. We ask the farmers what product they have too much of. By purchasing that product we not only help them out, but can also help consumers understand, and taste, how off-cuts, or "ugly" fruits and vegetables, can be used in creative ways. Once that light goes on, it's another boon to the farmers.

My love for foraging and preservation came later in my career, as I searched for new ways to apply everything I've learned since dicing onions for my mom. Understanding how much edible produce grows in the wild has been incredibly inspiring, and, with the help of numerous more experienced foragers, Keith and I are able to educate our guests on the bounty our region has to offer. Given the short "season" on many foraged goods, I also began reading a lot of different books and articles on preservation methods such as pickling, fermenting, and canning, a deep dive that opened my eyes to new flavors and textures.

I constantly push myself to learn and develop so that I can inspire those around me. By working with local products, Keith and I not only help farmers continue doing what they love and convey their riches to the community, we also gain a story to tell.

≡ A STORY IN EVERY BITE ≡

BY KEITH SARASIN

I STILL REMEMBER the first time I walked through the apple orchard in Hollis, New Hampshire. The smell of the crisp autumn air. The muddy ground, uneven after being trampled on by hundreds of eager pickers. The deep reds and greens in the rows of pristine trees. The chill as winter began its approach. I remember reaching up into the branches and twisting a fresh apple off a limb. I remember the slight crack as the tree released its fruit. These indelible childhood memories are ones that I cherish and long to share with others.

The story of my culinary journey starts with a confession. I feel guilty and terrible writing it, but I'm willing to bet she would have agreed: my mother wasn't the greatest cook. It became clear early on that I was much more interested in food and cooking than she was, and my first basic recipes came from an old 1950s cookbook that my grandmother had passed down to my mother. I butchered my first recipe, a batch of peanut butter cookies, but thankfully my mother uttered words of encouragement as she managed to choke down a bite or two.

I must have tried all of the recipes in that book at least a dozen times over the years. Through much trial and error I learned how combining simple ingredients can create outstanding flavors and textures.

As I grew older I was naturally drawn to the culinary scene, and my first big step on this journey was working as a line cook in various New Hampshire restaurants. It didn't take long for me to recognize a disconnect between the food I was preparing and the diners who were eating it. This wasn't an issue of variety or availability—there were plenty of companies offering a seemingly endless array of produce; and, being the only options as far as most were concerned, the restaurants flocked to these companies because of their low prices and convenient delivery options. I don't think that these companies, or the restaurants that purchased from them, had bad intentions. I just think that it was "business as usual." It wasn't a lack of choice or a matter of principle that caused these restaurants to source their food from hundreds or thousands of miles away, it was plain ignorance. Many simply didn't know that farmers were already producing high-quality food in their area. Those who did assumed it would be too complicated or expensive to use fresh, local produce. Once I realized that these misconceptions existed, I became interested in finding alternative ways to source ingredients, and it was this desire that began my journey to empower hometown farmers and help people learn to appreciate local food.

The concept for The Farmers Dinner started in a bar in downtown Nashua, New Hampshire. Every Wednesday, I had the opportunity to take over the place and cook local food for local people. We brought in local musicians, a local bartender who grew up on a farm, and some seasonally inspired specials. We promoted it with social media and people slowly came to appreciate what we were doing. I remember sitting in the bar after one of our Wednesday events thinking about how much fun this would be out on an actual farm, even though I couldn't imagine how to cook in a field where there is no running water or electricity. It was a fantasy, but one that would eventually lead me down a path that changed my life and the lives of many people in my community.

The first official Farmers Dinner took place in June 2012, in an upscale restaurant. The concept was simple; we wanted to source as many products locally as we could, and in between courses have farmers get up and share a story about their work. My hope was that if people heard the stories of these farmers and got to shake hands with them, maybe we could help people reconnect with their local farms, and their food. But I needed farmers. So I approached the farm stand at Kimball Fruit Farm in Pepperell, Massachusetts, on a hot summer day. I had no money in my bank account and had only hosted a couple of events at the bar in Nashua. But I was about to ask the farmer to donate some food to this event. Carl Hills, the owner of Kimball Fruit Farm, met me with a firm handshake. Thankfully, my enthusiasm was strong enough to make itself clear, because I stammered through my elevator pitch. Carl saw something in me that day that I couldn't have, and agreed to provide us with some of his produce. After that first ask, the others were much easier.

The evening of the event, I was nervous. I threw on an old sport coat I'd purchased from a thrift store and walked into the restaurant. To my surprise, we were at capacity for the evening. The actual service was a blur of nerves and excitement, and at the end of night people were smiling ear to ear. Several people wanted to know about the next one. They wanted to bring their friends. The restaurant was happy, the farmers were happy, and the customers were thrilled. We agreed to throw one more event three months later. This time it sold out in 24 hours and we had a 110-person waiting list.

Ideas don't make businesses and if it wasn't for a local marketing expert and a friend of mine, I'm not sure I would be writing these words. Early on, when we realized we had a great idea, we needed to figure out the best way to convert that idea into a business. The success we enjoy today stems from following the three core tenets that we established early on:

1. It had to be a win for the farmer. We couldn't take donations because that defeated the entire purpose of supporting local farmers. So, after that first event, we have never again taken a donation.

2. It had to be a win for the customer. We wanted the customer to have a memorable experience. People can choose to dine at any number of restaurants. Our events are about the food, to be sure, but we also aim to educate and inspire customers through the menus we prepare and the stories of those we partner with.

3. It had to be a win for us. We needed to make money and grow to continue with the dinners.

As time went on, I learned to "speak farmer," as did my team. Speaking farmer meant internalizing growing cycles, understanding seasons, and learning to order during processing dates. By doing so, we became a part of the farm. As we began to grow we'd spend anywhere from 5 to 10 hours on each and every farm we worked with, assisting them and cooking for them. These farms weren't just our business partners, they were friends and neighbors, people we grew to love. There are countless stories of us helping farmers catch a cow that broke free, mending fences, moving flocks of turkeys, and pitching in with the daily chores. Much of our success has been predicated on our unyielding determination to show up and get involved. We weren't just throwing farm-to-table events, we were bringing tables and helping hands to farms across New England.

During this time, I became a sort of ambassador for the local food scene. I was asked to judge a food competition. The competition gave contestants 1 hour to prepare a dish using what was available in a mystery basket of local ingredients, and Chris was the second chef we were judging. When you have been in the industry for a long time, you can get a sense rather quickly for the quality of a chef's work by looking at their station. Before I even saw what he did with one of the mystery ingredients we were giving the chefs, I knew Chris was special. His station was clean, his knives were sharp, and his attention to detail was first-rate. Chris won the competition that day and we stayed in touch. Eventually, I invited him to be the guest chef at one of my dinners. Able to watch him up close, I found his approach incredibly inspiring. And our guests were enchanted by the remarkable dishes he turned out.

Chris joined The Farmers Dinner team in 2017 and our friendship has since flourished. We would eagerly spend hours together foraging, learning, and hanging out with farmers. I was constantly in awe of his talent in the kitchen and his attention to even the smallest detail. I could not ask for a better friend, mentor, and business partner. He is a shining example of how this industry can drive people to greatness. His food has continually humbled and

inspired me and I am honored to work by his side. Thanks to our time together at The Farmers Dinner, we decided to open Greenleaf, a rustic, farm-to-table restaurant in Milford, New Hampshire.

Chris and I, along with the rest of The Farmers Dinner team, have met countless men and women who've shared their stories, both good and bad. We have hosted events in fields, shut down Main Streets, thrown dinners in wineries, distilleries, and old barns; we've become stewards of the land and, best of all, inspired others to do the same. People have met at our events and forged friendships, relationships, even a marriage. As of 2018, we have hosted 75 events, given over $115,000 back to local farmers, and served 15,385 customers.

When you come to a Farmers Dinner event, you can expect a unique experience. In over 370 courses, we have never repeated a single dish. These recipes are inspired by the farms we have worked with, the changing seasons, and the passion and dedication that we have put into our food over the years.

Thank you to everyone who has worked with us, inspired us, visited us, and cared for us. You are the reason we are able to write this book. After countless hours spent with farmers and customers, I've learned that there really is a story in every bite.

Otis 4.30.17
1) Braised Leek — Hard Sear
   - Texture — Crunchy Garlic & Shallot
   - Pickled Ramps   onion
   - Black Garlic Ranch   Sprout
   - Chive Bubbles — Versa Whip
   - Chive Blossom/Bk Onion Sauce
     Cold oil Mandarin Garlic chip
     Sauce oil

2) Pea
      Shoots & Tendrils → ½ Pound
   - Ricotta Gnocchi
   - Ham Powder / Bacon Broth
   - Snap Peas
   - Green Apricot Mostarda
     (Brine Pickled Mustard Seed)

Farmers DINNER

BULLY BOY
DISTILLERS

BOSTON

Smoked Potato Soup
Nasturtium, Vodka, Brookford Farm Cheddar

Lamb Sausage Momo's
Spent Grain & Chili Chutney

* First 2 Courses: Paired with Planter's Punch
White Rum, Boston Rum, House Grenadine, Bitters.

Striped Bass
Kumquat, Seaweed, Rhubarb

Fried Oyster Sandwich
*Pickled Meyer Lemon, Ramp Kewpi,
Squid Ink Bun*

* 3rd & 4th Courses: Paired with Lime Rickey
Estate Gin, Simple, Lime, Soda, Hub Punch Float.

Pork Head Tostada
*Whiskey Mole, Wolf Meadow Caciotta,
Heirloom Corn Chip*

"Old Fashion" Ice Cream Sundae
Orange, Bourbon, Bitters

* 5th & 6th Courses: Paired with Barrel Aged Boston Rum Old
Fashioned.

THE PARLOR   **Digging for Roots**

SPRING

· BEES TO BUDS ·

≡ SPRING ≡

IN LATE MARCH, Chris and I will arrive at Kimball Fruit Farm in Pepperell, Massachusetts, and be greeted by the smiling face of Carl Hills, the owner and farmer. Carl will tell us to jump in his old Silverado and take us all around the farm for a tour. Each year, he explains what's looking good in terms of produce and how the previous winter will impact the growing season. These annual visits have become roadmaps for us, guiding us toward innovative and creative dishes. Years after the first spring trip to Carl's farm, we hosted a 150-person dinner there, and named the courses after sections of the farm, like "Upper Greenhouse," "The Lower Field," and "Berry Patch."

Spring bestows a profound sense of rebirth upon New England. For the farms, it is the start of a long year ahead, filled with promise and hope. Farms are busy planting seeds, tending to the greenhouses, and tilling fields.

For the consumer, it is a chance to reconnect with the community. After a long winter, people are itching to get outside and feel the sun's warmth once again. We long for fresh food. Gone are the days of stews and heavy, hearty dishes. Now is the time for fresh greens, asparagus, herbs, and the sour tang of rhubarb to emerge—marking the return to a lighter style of eating.

For the chef, spring is a clean slate, which means it's time to revamp menus. The inevitable spring menu change comes with considerable excitement.

At The Farmers Dinner, we deal with micro-seasons. A micro-season is a short snapshot of availability during the course of a growing cycle. For instance, with the local farms we work with, there are roughly 4 to 5 weeks of asparagus during the year. When you think about a year having 52 weeks, and for 4 of those weeks you get perfect asparagus, you can imagine how excited we get about a particular micro-season.

Spring is also challenging. People want to jump to what is available in supermarkets. Just because it is a "spring item" doesn't mean it is available at local farms. This is why we love to visit farms, get our hands on the produce, and plan accordingly. When you have short growing seasons you learn very quickly to preserve the season. This means pickling ramps, canning asparagus, and fermenting fiddleheads.

With spring we also rekindle our romance with foraging: morels pop up on lawns across the region, black locust flowers bloom for one week only, wood sorrel is abundant once again, sumac shoots start to sprout.

From its vitality to the endless calls for creativity, spring never ceases to inspire and provide exactly what is needed after the long winter.

RUSTIC WHOLE WHEAT BREAD

MY BREAD–BAKING JOURNEY BEGAN 2 YEARS AGO, when rustic-style loaves caught my attention. After reading many books and experimenting on my own, I certainly have a newfound appreciation for bread making and the artisans who have mastered it, as it requires total investment. That said, I can still turn out some tasty loaves, as this recipe shows.—*C.V.*

YIELD: 1 LOAF ⋯ **ACTIVE TIME: 30 MINUTES** ⋯ **TOTAL TIME: 21 HOURS**

350 g all-purpose flour, plus more for dusting

150 g whole wheat flour

375 g water (90°F)

500 mg active dry yeast (just under ¼ teaspoon)

11 g salt

1 Place the flours and water in a large mixing bowl and use your hands to combine the mixture into a dough. Cover the bowl with a kitchen towel and let the mixture set for 45 minutes to 1 hour.

2 Sprinkle the yeast and salt over the dough and fold until they have been incorporated. Cover the bowl with the kitchen towel and let stand for 30 minutes. Remove the towel, fold a corner of the dough into the center, and cover. Repeat every 30 minutes until all of the corners have been folded in.

3 After the last fold, cover the dough with the kitchen towel and let it sit for 12 to 14 hours.

4 Dust a work surface lightly with flour and place the dough on it. Fold each corner of the dough to the center, flip the dough over, and roll it into a smooth ball. Dust your hands with flour as needed. Be careful not to roll or press the dough too hard, as this will prevent the dough from expanding properly. Dust a bowl with flour and place the dough, seam side down, in the bowl. Let stand until it has roughly doubled in size, about 1 hour and 15 minutes.

5 Cut a round piece of parchment paper that is 1" larger than the circumference of your Dutch oven. When the dough has approximately 1 hour left in its rise (this is also known as "proofing"), preheat the oven to 475°F and place the covered Dutch oven in the oven as it warms.

6 When the dough has roughly doubled in size, invert it onto a lightly floured work surface. Use a very sharp knife to score one side of the loaf. Using oven mitts, remove the Dutch oven from the oven. Use a bench scraper to transfer the dough onto the piece of parchment. Hold the sides of the parchment and carefully lower the dough into the Dutch oven. Cover the Dutch oven and place it in the oven for 20 minutes.

7 Remove the Dutch oven's lid and bake the loaf for an additional 20 minutes. Remove from the oven and let cool on a wire rack for at least 2 hours before slicing.

NOTE: Due to the precision required in bread making, we elected to use the metric system for the artisanal bread recipes in the book.

PEA SHOOT PESTO

PEA SHOOTS ARE THE YOUNG SHOOTS OF PEAS. They have a clean and fresh flavor that lends itself wonderfully to pesto. When I make this, I try to prepare enough that I can preserve a couple of jars and hold on to that taste all year long.—*K.S.*

YIELD: 2 CUPS ◦→ **ACTIVE TIME: 15 MINUTES** →◦→ **TOTAL TIME: 15 MINUTES**

2 cups pea shoots

1 cup basil leaves

2 tablespoons fresh lemon juice

½ teaspoon red pepper flakes

¼ cup pine nuts

¼ cup grated Parmesan cheese

¼ cup olive oil

Salt and pepper, to taste

1   Place the pea shoots, basil, lemon juice, red pepper flakes, pine nuts, and Parmesan in a food processor and pulse until you have a rough paste. Slowly add the olive oil as you continue to pulse the mixture.

2   Season with salt and pepper. Store in an airtight container in the refrigerator if preparing ahead of time, or can to preserve for a longer period of time.

ASPARAGUS WITH PANCETTA
& GARLIC CREAM SAUCE

ASPARAGUS HAS A UNIQUE, EARTHY FLAVOR that teams with the richness of pancetta and the creamy garlic sauce to produce this well-rounded dish.—*K.S.*

YIELD: 4 SERVINGS   ⋅→⋅   **ACTIVE TIME: 20 MINUTES**   ⋅→⋅   **TOTAL TIME: 35 MINUTES**

Salt and pepper, to taste

2 bunches of asparagus

3 garlic cloves, minced

2 cups heavy cream

3 tablespoons unsalted butter

1 tablespoon cornstarch

1 cup diced pancetta

1   Bring a pot of salted water to a boil. While waiting for the water to boil, remove the woody, white parts of the asparagus and discard them.

2   When the water is boiling, add the asparagus and cook until tender, about 2 minutes. Drain and set aside.

3   Place the garlic, cream, and butter in a medium saucepan and bring to a simmer over medium heat. Stir in the cornstarch to thicken sauce.

4   Place the pancetta in a skillet and cook over medium-high heat until it turns a light golden brown. Add the pancetta to the garlic-and-cream mixture and stir to combine. Season with salt and pepper, pour over the asparagus, and serve.

ROASTED ASPARAGUS WITH SUNNY-SIDE EGGS & LEMON-PEPPER MAYONNAISE

FOR A CHEF, THE MOST EXCITING THING about seeing flowers return in the spring is knowing that asparagus season is right around the corner. This side dish is perfect for a bright spring day, and is wonderful with or without the eggs.—*CV.*

YIELD: 4 TO 6 SERVINGS ⋯ **ACTIVE TIME: 20 MINUTES** ⋯ **TOTAL TIME: 35 MINUTES**

FOR THE ASPARAGUS & EGGS

Salt and pepper, to taste

2 bunches of asparagus

2 tablespoons olive oil

2 tablespoons unsalted butter

6 eggs

Grated Parmesan cheese, for garnish

FOR THE MAYONNAISE

1 cup mayonnaise

3 tablespoons grated Parmesan cheese

1 tablespoon lemon zest

3 tablespoons fresh lemon juice

½ tablespoon black pepper

2 teaspoons salt

1 Preheat the oven to 400°F.

2 Bring a large pot of salted water to a boil and prepare an ice water bath in a large bowl. Trim the woody ends of the asparagus and discard.

3 Place the trimmed asparagus in the boiling water and cook for 30 seconds. Drain and transfer to the ice water bath until completely cool, about 3 minutes. Transfer to a kitchen towel to dry completely.

4 Prepare the mayonnaise. Place all of the ingredients in a mixing bowl and whisk to combine. Set aside.

5 Pat the asparagus dry. Place the olive oil in a sauté pan and warm over medium-high heat. Just before the oil starts to smoke, add the asparagus in batches and cook until browned all over. Transfer cooked asparagus to a plate and tent with foil to keep warm.

6 Place the butter in a cast-iron skillet and melt over medium heat. Crack the eggs into the pan, taking care not to break the yolks. Season with salt and pepper and place the skillet in the oven. Cook until the whites are cooked through, 2 to 3 minutes. Remove from the oven.

7 To serve, spread some of the mayonnaise on a plate and lay some asparagus on top. Top with an egg and garnish with the grated Parmesan.

SPRING SALAD WITH GREEN GODDESS DRESSING

THE DIVINE MONIKER IS NO ACCIDENT—this dressing is thick and robust enough to lend body to this light salad, but delicate enough to keep you mindful of the fresh herbs that comprise it.—*C.V.*

YIELD: 4 SERVINGS ⤙ ⤚ **ACTIVE TIME: 20 MINUTES** ⤙ ⤚ **TOTAL TIME: 40 MINUTES**

FOR THE DRESSING

½ cup mayonnaise

⅔ cup buttermilk

1 tablespoon fresh lemon juice

2 tablespoons chopped celery leaves

2 tablespoons chopped parsley leaves

2 tablespoons chopped tarragon

2 tablespoons sliced chives

2 teaspoons salt

1 teaspoon black pepper

FOR THE SALAD

Salt and pepper, to taste

6 asparagus stalks, trimmed and chopped

4 oz. snap peas, trimmed and chopped

3 heads of baby red leaf lettuce, halved

3 radishes, sliced thin with a mandoline, for garnish

Celery leaves, for garnish

1 Prepare the dressing. Place all of the ingredients in a food processor and puree until thoroughly combined. Transfer to a container and place in the refrigerator until ready to serve.

2 Bring a pot of salted water to a boil and prepare an ice water bath in a large bowl. Place the asparagus in the boiling water, cook for 1 minute, remove with a strainer, and transfer to the water bath until completely cool. Drain and transfer to a kitchen towel to dry.

3 Let the water come back to a boil. Place the peas in the boiling water, cook for 1 minute, remove with a strainer, and transfer to the water bath until completely cool. Transfer to a kitchen towel to dry.

4 Place the halved heads of lettuce on the serving plates. Place the asparagus and peas in a bowl, season with salt and pepper, and add the dressing. Toss to combine and place on top of the lettuce. Drizzle with additional dressing and garnish with the radishes and celery leaves.

CONFIT NEW POTATOES

NEW POTATOES ARE YOUNG POTATOES that are pulled in early spring. They are sweeter than their mature counterparts, since the sugars haven't had time to develop into starches, and are so soft and tender that they don't need to be peeled.—*K.S.*

YIELD: 4 TO 6 SERVINGS ⟶ **ACTIVE TIME: 5 MINUTES** ⟶ **TOTAL TIME: 1 HOUR AND 10 MINUTES**

4 cups canola oil

5 lbs. new potatoes

Salt and pepper, to taste

1 Place the oil in a deep, heavy-bottomed pot and bring it to 200°F over medium heat.

2 While the oil is warming, wash the potatoes and pat them dry. Carefully place the potatoes in the oil and cook until fork tender, about 1 hour.

3 Drain the potatoes, season generously with salt and pepper, and stir to ensure that the potatoes are evenly coated.

NOTE: These potatoes should have plenty of flavor, but if you're looking to take them to another level, replace the canola oil with chicken or duck fat.

ROASTED OVER-WINTERED PARSNIPS WITH MAPLE BUTTER

OVER-WINTERED PARSNIPS REMAIN IN THE GROUND until the spring, and the freezing temperatures that they endure preserve the sugars so that they are packed with amazing sweetness and flavor by the time they are dug up. This recipe is also a nod to the hardworking sugar shacks across New England, as adding maple syrup to creamy butter provides another level of sweetness and depth to this dish.—*K.S.*

YIELD: 4 TO 6 SERVINGS •••• **ACTIVE TIME: 15 MINUTES** •••• **TOTAL TIME: 1 HOUR**

3 lbs. parsnips

2 tablespoons vegetable oil

Salt, to taste

½ cup local maple syrup

1 stick of unsalted butter, softened

1 Preheat the oven to 425°F.

2 Trim and halve the parsnips and rinse them well. Pat them dry, place on a baking sheet, drizzle with the vegetable oil, and season with salt.

3 Place the parsnips in the oven and bake until golden brown, about 30 to 40 minutes.

4 While the parsnips are in the oven, place the maple syrup and butter in a bowl and whip to combine. Season with salt and place in the refrigerator until ready to serve.

5 When the parsnips are done cooking, remove from the oven and transfer to a mixing bowl. Add the maple butter, stir until the parsnips are evenly coated, and serve.

SPICY BABY CARROTS WITH TOASTED SEED GRANOLA & HONEY–THYME YOGURT

THIS SPICE BLEND IS SIMILAR to what you would find in a barbecue rub. Not only does it work well with the sweet carrots, it's a nice reminder that warmer weather is straight ahead.—*CV.*

YIELD: 4 TO 6 SERVINGS ⟶ **ACTIVE TIME: 30 MINUTES** ⟶ **TOTAL TIME: 1 HOUR AND 45 MINUTES**

2 lbs. baby carrots

2 tablespoons olive oil

1½ tablespoons salt, plus 1½ teaspoons

1 teaspoon pepper

2 teaspoons cumin

1 teaspoon ground fennel seeds

1 teaspoon ground coriander seeds

1 teaspoon paprika

2 teaspoons brown sugar

2 cups plain Greek yogurt

2 tablespoons honey

1½ teaspoons chopped thyme leaves, plus more for garnish

½ cup Toasted Seed Granola (see sidebar)

1 Preheat the oven to 375°F.

2 Wash and trim the carrots. Drain and pat dry.

3 Place the carrots, olive oil, 1½ tablespoons of salt, pepper, cumin, fennel, coriander, paprika, and brown sugar in a bowl and toss to coat evenly. Arrange the carrots in an even layer on a foil–lined baking sheet. Bake carrots in oven until tender, about 25 minutes. Remove and let cool slightly.

4 Place the yogurt, honey, remaining salt, and thyme in the serving dish and stir to combine. Place the carrots on top and sprinkle the granola over the carrots. Garnish with additional thyme.

NOTE: If using multiple colors of carrots to enhance the presentation, prepare to season and roast them separately as the purple variety will bleed and color the others.

TOASTED SEED GRANOLA

YIELD: 2½ CUPS · ACTIVE TIME: 10 MINUTES
TOTAL TIME: 1 HOUR

1 tablespoon maple syrup
2 tablespoons honey
2 tablespoons brown sugar
2 tablespoons vegetable oil
1 teaspoon salt
1½ cups oats
½ cup dried cranberries
¾ cup toasted squash seeds

1   Preheat the oven to 300°F. Place the syrup, honey, brown sugar, oil, and salt in a small saucepan and warm over medium heat, stirring, until the sugar has dissolved.

2   Place the oats in a mixing bowl, add the honey mixture, and stir until the oats are evenly coated. Transfer to a parchment–lined baking sheet, place it in the oven, and bake for 40 minutes, stirring the mixture every 10 minutes to ensure it bakes evenly.

3   Remove from the oven and let cool slightly. Transfer to a mixing bowl, fold in the cranberries and toasted seeds, and serve.

BRAISED LAMB SHOULDER WITH MINTY PEAS

THIS RECIPE CAME ABOUT after a conversation with a farmer named Jim Czack, who raises Black Welsh lamb on Loudonshire Farm in Loudon, New Hampshire. I was looking for lamb with a good protein-to-fat ratio and exceptional flavor. Jim let me know that the superior quality of the Black Welsh's meat was the answer to my prayers. After experimenting with it briefly, I landed on this simple recipe.—*K.S.*

YIELD: 4 TO 6 SERVINGS ⇢ ACTIVE TIME: 30 MINUTES ⇢ TOTAL TIME: 4 HOURS

---

2 tablespoons canola oil

5-lb., bone-in lamb shoulder

Salt, to taste

1 small onion, diced

2 carrots, peeled and diced

3 bay leaves

2 tablespoons black peppercorns

2 cups water

2 sprigs of rosemary

3 sprigs of mint

3 cups peas

1 Preheat the oven to 300°F. Add the canola oil to a large skillet and warm it over medium-high heat. Season all sides of the lamb shoulder liberally with salt. When the oil starts to glisten, place the lamb in the pan and cook, while turning occasionally, until it is brown on all sides.

2 Place the onion, carrots, bay leaves, peppercorns, water, and rosemary in a Dutch oven or baking dish. When the lamb shoulder is browned all over, place it in the Dutch oven or baking dish, cover, and cook in the oven until the lamb is fork tender, approximately 3½ hours.

3 When the lamb shoulder is close to ready, place the sprigs of mint and peas in a saucepan and cover with water. Cook over medium heat until the peas are tender, approximately 4 minutes for fresh peas and 7 minutes if using frozen. Drain, discard the sprigs of mint, and serve alongside the lamb shoulder.

GRILLED LAMB LOIN WITH QUINOA
& RADISH LEAF CHIMICHURRI

AFTER THE LONG WINTER the first thing I want to do when the sun is warm and shining is fire up the grill. This dish is inspired by that urge, but it is also a lighter entrée that will seem extra special after the stream of heavy meals consumed during the winter.—*C.V.*

YIELD: 6 SERVINGS → **ACTIVE TIME: 45 MINUTES** → **TOTAL TIME: 3 HOURS AND 30 MINUTES**

FOR THE LAMB & QUINOA

2½-lb. lamb loin

½ cup Lamb Marinade (see sidebar)

2 cups quinoa

4½ cups water

1 small shallot, trimmed and halved

2 teaspoons salt, plus more to taste

6 heads of baby bok choy, trimmed

10 radishes, trimmed and quartered, tops reserved

Pepper, to taste

½ cup White Wine Vinaigrette (see sidebar)

FOR THE CHIMICHURRI

1 small shallot, minced

2 garlic cloves, minced

¼ teaspoon red pepper flakes

¼ cup red wine vinegar

⅔ cup chopped radish leaves

1 tablespoon oregano

½ cup olive oil

2 teaspoons salt, plus more to taste

1   Trim the fat from the lamb loin. Rub with the marinade and let it marinate in the refrigerator for at least 2 hours. Remove approximately 45 minutes prior to grilling.

2   Place the quinoa in a fine sieve and run under cold water until the water runs clear. Place the quinoa in a medium saucepan and cover with the water. Add the shallot and salt and bring to a boil. Cover and lower the temperature so that the quinoa simmers. Cook until all of the liquid has been absorbed, about 20 minutes. Remove the shallot, spread the quinoa in an even layer on a baking sheet, and let cool.

3   Bring a pot of salted water to bowl. Prepare an ice water bath in a medium-sized bowl. Rinse the bok choy under cold water and place them in the boiling water. Cook for 1 minute, remove with a strainer, and transfer to the water bath.

4   Let the water come back to a boil and then add the radish tops. Cook for 1 minute, remove with a strainer, and transfer to the water bath. When the vegetables have cooled completely, drain, pat dry, and place them in a mixing bowl. Season with salt and pepper, add the quartered radishes and vinaigrette, and toss to evenly coat. Set aside.

5   Preheat your gas or charcoal grill to 450°F. Place the lamb loin on the grill and cook, while turning, until the loin is seared on all sides and the internal temperature is 140°F. Remove from the grill and let sit for 10 minutes before slicing.

6   Prepare the chimichurri. Place all of the ingredients in a mixing bowl and whisk until combined. Season to taste and set aside.

7   To serve, place quinoa and dressed vegetables on a plate and top with slices of the lamb loin. Drizzle with the chimichurri or serve it on the side.

LAMB MARINADE

YIELD: 1¼ CUPS • ACTIVE TIME: 5 MINUTES
TOTAL TIME: 5 MINUTES

8 garlic cloves, minced

1 tablespoon cumin

2 tablespoons pepper

1 tablespoon ground fennel seeds

1 tablespoon paprika

2 tablespoons salt

2 teaspoons Dijon mustard

1 cup olive oil

Place all of the ingredients in a mixing bowl and stir until combined.

WHITE WINE VINAIGRETTE

YIELD: ½ CUP • ACTIVE TIME: 5 MINUTES
TOTAL TIME: 5 MINUTES

2 tablespoons white wine vinegar

2 teaspoons whole grain mustard

1 tablespoon honey

1 tablespoon sliced chives

2 teaspoons chopped thyme leaves

2 teaspoons salt

¼ cup olive oil

Place all of the ingredients, except for the olive oil, in a mixing bowl and stir until well combined. Add the olive oil in a slow stream and stir until incorporated.

CREAMED ASPARAGUS SOUP
WITH BUTTERMILK & GARLIC CHIPS

THE FARMS WE WORK WITH ARE NOW HOME to many fond memories, and some of my absolute favorites reside at Kimball Fruit Farm. Their asparagus is typically ready in late April, before their farm stand opens for the season, so they set up shop and sell their asparagus right across from the patch. Each year, I purchase some and then walk across the street, pluck a stalk from the ground, and eat it right there. I wanted to recreate that exhilarating freshness in a dish, and this soup is the result of those efforts.—*K.S.*

YIELD: 4 TO 6 SERVINGS ⋯ **ACTIVE TIME: 30 MINUTES** ⋯ **TOTAL TIME: 1 HOUR**

2 bunches of asparagus

4 tablespoons unsalted butter

1 small onion, diced

4 cups Chicken Stock (see page 236)

1 cup canola oil

4 garlic cloves, sliced very thin using a mandoline

Salt, to taste

½ cup buttermilk, for garnish

1 Cut off the tips of the asparagus and set them aside. Cut off the white, woody ends of the asparagus and discard. Cut what remains of the stalks into 2-inch pieces.

2 Melt the butter in a medium saucepan over medium-low heat. Add the onion and sauté until it is soft and translucent, about 6 minutes.

3 Add the stock and 2-inch pieces of asparagus to the saucepan, raise the heat to medium, and simmer for 20 minutes.

4 Place the canola oil in a Dutch oven and bring it to 350°F over medium-high heat. Place the thinly sliced garlic in the oil, cook until golden brown, and then place on a paper towel–lined plate to drain.

5 Bring a small pot of salted water to a boil and then add the asparagus tips. Cook for approximately 2 minutes, drain, and set aside.

6 Once the soup has simmered for 20 minutes, transfer to a blender and puree until smooth. Pour into warmed bowls, season to taste, and garnish each bowl with a drizzle of buttermilk, the asparagus tips, and the garlic chips.

NOTE: Make sure to vent the blender when pureeing this soup and other hot liquids. Otherwise pressure can build and leave you with a real mess.

SPRING PEA SOUP WITH LEMON RICOTTA

EARLY IN THE SPRING, peas are absolutely perfect—tender enough that they don't require a long cook time and bursting with country fresh flavor. Pair them with mint and creamy, zesty ricotta, and you've got a dish that positively sings.—*E.V.*

YIELD: 4 SERVINGS ⟶ **ACTIVE TIME: 15 MINUTES** ⟶ **TOTAL TIME: 25 MINUTES**

1 cup ricotta cheese

¼ cup heavy cream

2 tablespoons grated lemon zest, plus 6 strips

2 tablespoons salt, plus 2 teaspoons

12 cups water

3 cups peas

3 small shallots, diced

6 mint leaves, plus more for garnish

1 Place the ricotta, cream, grated lemon zest, and 2 teaspoons of salt in a food processor and puree until smooth. Season to taste and set aside.

2 Place the water and remaining salt in a saucepan and bring to a boil over medium heat. Place the strips of lemon zest in the saucepan with the peas and shallots. Cook for 2 to 3 minutes, until the peas are just cooked through. Drain, reserve 2 cups of the cooking liquid, and immediately transfer the peas, strips of lemon zest, and shallots to a blender. Add the mint leaves and half of the reserved cooking liquid and puree until the desired consistency is achieved, adding more cooking liquid as needed.

3 Season to taste, ladle into warmed bowls, and place a spoonful of the lemon ricotta in each bowl. Garnish with additional mint and serve immediately, as the soup's brilliant green color starts to fade as it cools.

LEFTOVER CHICKEN SALAD

CHRIS AND I HATE FOOD WASTE. Holding large dinners on farms forces us to get creative and find exciting ways to utilize items that are left over from prep. This chicken salad is just one product of those endeavors, and while it may be simple, it is packed with flavor.—*K.S.*

YIELD: 4 TO 6 SERVINGS ◦•◦ **ACTIVE TIME: 20 MINUTES** ◦•◦ **TOTAL TIME: 20 MINUTES**

½ cup mayonnaise

½ cup chopped celery

1 spring onion, chopped

1 teaspoon mustard

½ teaspoon fresh lemon juice

2 to 3 cups of leftover roasted chicken, diced or shredded

¼ cup walnuts or pecans (optional)

Salt and pepper, to taste

Sourdough Bread
(see page 147), sliced

1 Place the mayonnaise, celery, spring onion, mustard, and lemon juice in a mixing bowl and stir to combine.

2 Add the chicken and, if desired, the nuts. Season with salt and pepper and serve on the slices of bread.

COTTAGE PIE

MOST PEOPLE ARE FAMILIAR with shepherd's pie. This riff uses lamb and peas to ramp up the flavor, and it is perfect for those spring days when the chill of winter creeps back in and you need a hearty dish to keep your spirits up.—*K.S.*

YIELD: 4 TO 6 SERVINGS ◦•◦ **ACTIVE TIME: 20 MINUTES** ◦•◦ **TOTAL TIME: 1 HOUR AND 30 MINUTES**

1 tablespoon canola oil

1 tablespoon unsalted butter

1 spring onion, diced

1 lb. ground lamb

1 tablespoon fresh minced thyme leaves

1 cup beef or lamb stock

1 cup peas

5 potatoes, peeled, cooked, and mashed

Salt and pepper, to taste

1 Preheat the oven to 350°F. Place the canola oil and butter in a cast-iron skillet and warm over medium-high heat. Add the onion and sauté until lightly golden brown, about 4 minutes.

2 Add the lamb and thyme and cook, while stirring, until the lamb is browned.

3 Add the stock, reduce the heat to medium-low, and let the mixture gently simmer until the stock has nearly evaporated, about 20 minutes.

4 Add the peas to the skillet, stir to combine, and cook until warmed through.

5 Transfer the mixture from the skillet to a baking dish. Season the mashed potatoes with salt and pepper and then cover the lamb-and-peas mixture with the potatoes. Smooth the top with a rubber spatula and bake in the oven until the top is golden brown, about 40 minutes. Remove from the oven and serve.

TAGLIATELLE WITH ASPARAGUS AND PEAS

ONE OF MY FAVORITE THINGS to make is fresh pasta, as it offers a variety of shapes and flavors, and allows even the most modest dishes to prove satisfying. Making your own pasta may seem daunting, but trust me: it's far easier than you think.—*C.V.*

YIELD: 4 TO 6 SERVINGS ••• **ACTIVE TIME: 50 MINUTES** ••• **TOTAL TIME: 1 HOUR AND 30 MINUTES**

1½ cups all-purpose flour, plus more for dusting

1½ teaspoons salt

¾ cup egg yolks

1 tablespoon olive oil

1 bunch of asparagus, trimmed and chopped

½ lb. snap peas, trimmed and chopped

4 tablespoons unsalted butter

¼ cup grated Parmesan cheese

½ teaspoon red pepper flakes

1 Place the flour and salt in a mixing bowl, stir to combine, and make a well in the center. Pour the egg yolks and olive oil into the well and, starting in the center and gradually working to the outside, incorporate the flour into the well. When all the flour has been incorporated, place the dough on a lightly floured work surface and knead until it is a smooth ball. Wrap it in plastic and let rest for at least 30 minutes.

2 Divide the dough into quarters. Use a rolling pin to flatten each quarter to a thickness that can go through the widest setting on a pasta maker.

3 Run the rolled pieces of dough through the pasta maker, adjusting the setting to reduce the thickness with each pass. Roll until you can see your hand through the dough. Cut the sheets into 10-inch-long pieces, dust them with flour, stack them on top of each other, and gently roll them up. Cut the roll into ¼-inch-wide strips, unroll, and place the strips on baking sheets lightly dusted with flour.

4 Bring salted water to a boil in a medium saucepan and in a large saucepan. Place the asparagus and peas in the medium saucepan and cook for 1 minute. Drain and set aside.

5 Place the pasta in the large saucepan and cook for 3 to 4 minutes while stirring constantly. Before draining, reserve ¼ cup of the pasta water.

6 Place the butter in a large sauté pan and melt over medium heat. Add the pasta and vegetables and toss to combine. Add the pasta water, Parmesan, and red pepper flakes and toss to evenly coat. Season to taste and serve.

CHERRY PIE

ONE OF THE FIRST FRUITS TO COME UP IN NEW ENGLAND is the cherry, and I have so many memories of picking cherries off the trees at Kimball Fruit Farm. This pie is a proper tribute to the farm and the season.—*K.S.*

YIELD: 4 TO 6 SERVINGS   ⟶   **ACTIVE TIME: 30 MINUTES**   ⟶   **TOTAL TIME: 1 HOUR AND 30 MINUTES**

4 cups cherries
(dark or Rainier preferred), pitted

2 cups sugar

2 tablespoons fresh lemon juice

3 tablespoons cornstarch

1 tablespoon water

¼ teaspoon almond extract

2 Leaf Lard Piecrusts (see page 262)

1 egg, beaten

1 Preheat oven to 350°F. Place the cherries, sugar, and lemon juice in a saucepan and cook, while stirring occasionally, over medium heat until the mixture is syrupy.

2 Combine the cornstarch and water in a small bowl and stir this mixture into the saucepan. Reduce heat to low and cook, while stirring, until the mixture is thick. Remove from heat, add the almond extract, and let cool.

3 When the cherry mixture has cooled, place the bottom crust in a greased 9" pie plate and pour the cherry mixture into the crust. Top with the other crust, make a few slits in the top, and brush the top crust with the beaten egg.

4 Place the pie in the oven and bake until the top crust is golden brown, about 45 minutes. Remove and let cool before serving.

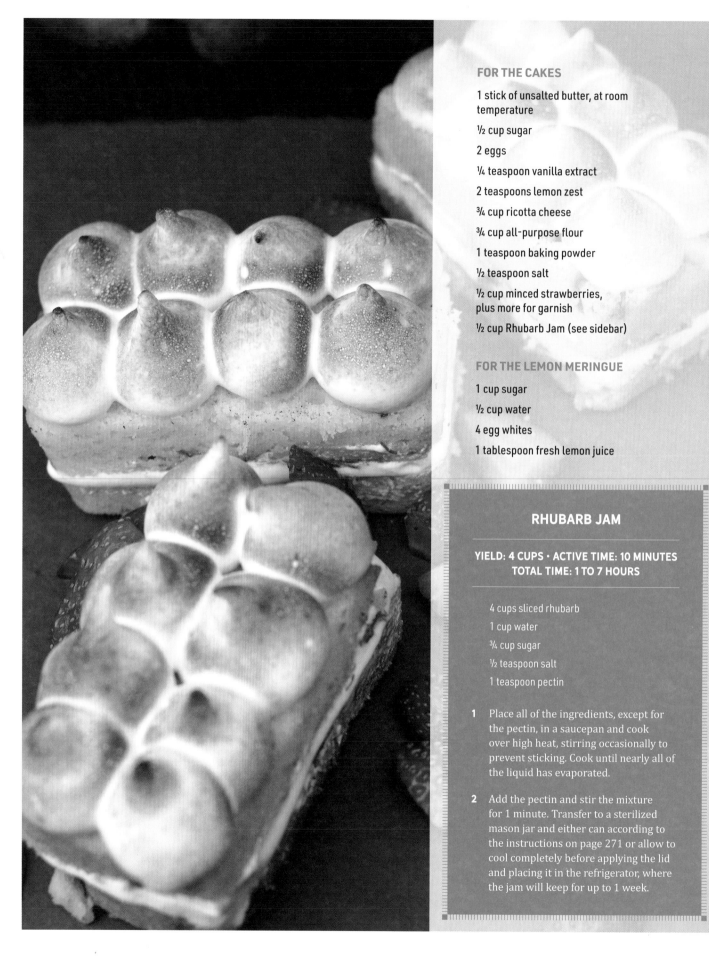

FOR THE CAKES

1 stick of unsalted butter, at room temperature

½ cup sugar

2 eggs

¼ teaspoon vanilla extract

2 teaspoons lemon zest

¾ cup ricotta cheese

¾ cup all-purpose flour

1 teaspoon baking powder

½ teaspoon salt

½ cup minced strawberries, plus more for garnish

½ cup Rhubarb Jam (see sidebar)

FOR THE LEMON MERINGUE

1 cup sugar

½ cup water

4 egg whites

1 tablespoon fresh lemon juice

RHUBARB JAM

YIELD: 4 CUPS · ACTIVE TIME: 10 MINUTES
TOTAL TIME: 1 TO 7 HOURS

4 cups sliced rhubarb

1 cup water

¾ cup sugar

½ teaspoon salt

1 teaspoon pectin

1   Place all of the ingredients, except for the pectin, in a saucepan and cook over high heat, stirring occasionally to prevent sticking. Cook until nearly all of the liquid has evaporated.

2   Add the pectin and stir the mixture for 1 minute. Transfer to a sterilized mason jar and either can according to the instructions on page 271 or allow to cool completely before applying the lid and placing it in the refrigerator, where the jam will keep for up to 1 week.

STRAWBERRY–RHUBARB RICOTTA CAKES
WITH LEMON MERINGUE

THE IDEA FOR THIS LIGHT SPIN ON A TRADITIONAL strawberry shortcake occurred to me near the end of spring, when rhubarb season is coming to a close and strawberries are just beginning to ripen.—*E.V.*

YIELD: 4 SERVINGS ⟶ **ACTIVE TIME: 30 MINUTES** ⟶ **TOTAL TIME: 1 HOUR AND 15 MINUTES**

1 Preheat the oven to 350°F. Place the butter and sugar in the mixing bowl of a stand mixer fitted with the paddle attachment and beat on high until the mixture is smooth and a pale yellow. Reduce speed to medium, add the eggs one at a time, and beat until incorporated. Add the vanilla, lemon zest, and ricotta and beat until the mixture is smooth.

2 Place the flour, baking powder, and salt in a mixing bowl and whisk to combine. Reduce the speed of the mixer to low, add the dry mixture, and beat until incorporated. Scrape the mixing bowl as needed while mixing the batter.

3 Add the strawberries and fold to incorporate. Grease four mini-cake pans, divide the batter between them, place them in the oven, and bake until a toothpick inserted into the centers of the cakes comes out clean, about 35 minutes. Remove from the oven and let cool to room temperature in the pan.

4 Prepare the meringue. Place the sugar and water in a saucepan and cook on high until the mixture is 240°F. While the simple syrup is heating up, place the egg whites and lemon juice in the mixing bowl of the stand mixer, now fitted with the whisk attachment. Beat at medium speed until soft peaks form, about 2 to 3 minutes.

5 When the simple syrup reaches 240°F, slowly add it to the beaten egg whites with the mixer running. Raise the speed to high and beat until stiff peaks form. To test whether the meringue is ready, remove the whisk attachment and turn it so that the whisk is facing up. The meringue should hold its shape. If desired, transfer the meringue to a pastry bag fitted with a piping tip.

6 Remove the cooled cakes from the pans and cut the tops off to create a flat surface. Starting at the vertical midpoint, cut each cake into 2 even layers. Spread some of the Rhubarb Jam over four of the pieces. Cover the jam with some of the meringue and then place the unadorned pieces of cake on top. Spread more meringue on top and toast with a pastry torch until golden brown. Garnish with additional strawberries and serve.

Kimball Farm   8-4-18

Lower Field — Brassica

Greenhouse — Cucumber, Zuccini

High Tunnel — Tomato

Upper Field

~~Foraged !~~

⑤ Jamaica — Duo ↑ Pork
Jerk Chicken & Calaloo

Preserved Fruit —

Berries — Dessert.

DINNER

Élevage de Volailles

July 23nd 2017

Menu

Black Mountain Welsh Sh

White Pekin Duck

Bean Feijoada & Maine Go

Naan bread

Pozole & Fermented Cabba

Ratatouille & stuffed squ

Mixed squash, currants &

Chocolate-vanilla cake with
and roasted peaches and

SUMMER

· STONE FRUITS TO STEAMERS ·

⩵ SUMMER ⩵

NEW ENGLAND summers are adventure filled. From fishing excursions to berry-scented fields packed with perfectly ripe fruit, summer is too rife with enjoyable options and far too quick, so we have to jam in as much as we can.

In 2017, we hosted an event on Butternut Farm in Farmington, New Hampshire. Weeks before the dinner the team was walking the farm and cultivating ideas. We stopped at the peach orchard and Anthony, a member of our staff, started asking about the varieties of peaches that the farm grew. As we walked down the path the sweet, fruity scent from the sun-kissed peach trees was intoxicating. I reached for a branch and twisted off a perfect peach. The moment my teeth sank into the tender flesh of the fruit, a burst of juice set off a thousand different sensations.

As we often use such flavor memories to construct our dishes, summer is filled with inspiration. From lobster to corn, stone fruits to berries, summer's abundance is seemingly limitless.

One of the challenges that we have as chefs is finding creative ways to highlight the strengths of a particular ingredient. We often remind our team: "Nature gave us this perfect item, our job is to not mess it up." We always want to recreate that experience from Butternut Farm in 2017. Doing this means looking outside the box to find methods that will still translate to the customer. This can mean buying bulk, overripe peaches and stewing them down for later use. Or using the pits to make a sour kombucha and then reducing it to a syrup.

Because of the season's ample bounty, we must consistently shift to reflect the micro-seasons that arise. Strawberries are a micro-season: typically lasting from the middle of June to the end of the month, these coveted berries force us to rethink our approach. Yes, they are delicious as is. But by making jam or dehydrating them, we can extend that micro-season a little longer.

To us, summer is a time to bask in the warmth of a moment. As you'll see in the recipes that follow, this applies to food on a number of levels.

RUSTIC WHITE BREAD

DON'T BE THROWN BY the "white" in the name. Letting the dough rest overnight allows an incredible amount of flavor to develop, resulting in a loaf that is anything but bland.—*C.V.*

YIELD: 1 LOAF ⋯ **ACTIVE TIME: 30 MINUTES** ⋯ **TOTAL TIME: 21 HOURS**

500 g all-purpose flour, plus more for dusting

375 g water (90°F)

500 mg yeast (just under ¼ teaspoon)

11 g salt

1 Place the flour and water in a large mixing bowl and use your hands to combine the mixture into a dough. Cover the bowl with a kitchen towel and let the mixture set for 45 minutes to 1 hour.

2 Sprinkle the yeast and salt over the dough and fold until they have been incorporated. Cover the bowl with the kitchen towel and let stand for 30 minutes. Remove the towel, fold a corner of the dough into the center, and cover. Repeat every 30 minutes until all of the corners have been folded in.

3 After the last fold, cover the dough with the kitchen towel and let it sit for 12 to 14 hours.

4 Dust a work surface lightly with flour and place the dough on it. Fold each corner of the dough to the center, flip the dough over, and roll it into a smooth ball. Dust your hands with flour as needed. Be careful not to roll or press the dough too hard, as this will prevent the dough from expanding properly. Dust a bowl with flour and place the dough, seam side down, in the bowl. Let stand until it has roughly doubled in size, about 1 hour and 15 minutes.

5 Cut a round piece of parchment paper that is 1" larger than the circumference of your Dutch oven. When the dough has approximately 1 hour left in its rise (this is also known as "proofing"), preheat the oven to 475°F and place the covered Dutch oven in the oven as it warms.

6 When the dough has roughly doubled in size, invert it onto a lightly floured work surface. Use a very sharp knife to score one side of the loaf. Using oven mitts, remove the Dutch oven from the oven. Use a bench scraper to transfer the dough onto the piece of parchment. Hold the sides of the parchment and carefully lower the dough into the Dutch oven. Cover the Dutch oven and place it in the oven for 20 minutes.

7 Remove the Dutch oven's lid and bake the loaf for an additional 20 minutes. Remove from the oven and let cool on a wire rack for at least 2 hours before slicing.

CORNBREAD WITH HONEY

I WAS INTRODUCED TO THE CONCEPT of adding a thick corn puree to a cornbread recipe at one of my first restaurant jobs. Though I've learned a whole lot since then, I've never found anything that tops that particular tip, as it adds a freshness straight cornmeal just can't approach.—*E.V.*

YIELD: 16 SERVINGS ⇢ **ACTIVE TIME: 40 MINUTES** ⇢ **TOTAL TIME: 2 HOURS AND 15 MINUTES**

5 ears of corn

10 tablespoons unsalted butter

1 cup diced onion

1 tablespoon minced garlic

2½ tablespoons salt, plus more to taste

2¾ cups heavy cream

2 cups all-purpose flour

2 cups cornmeal

¼ cup brown sugar

2 tablespoons baking powder

½ teaspoon cayenne pepper

½ teaspoon paprika

1½ cups honey

6 eggs

¼ cup sour cream

1   Preheat the oven to 400°F.

2   Place the ears of corn on a baking sheet, place it in the oven, and bake for 25 minutes, until the kernels have a slight give to them. Remove from the oven and let cool. When the ears of corn are cool enough to handle, remove the husks and silk and cut the kernels from the cob. Reserve the corn cobs for another preparation. Lower the oven temperature to 300°F.

3   Place 2 tablespoons of the butter in a large saucepan and melt over medium heat. Add the onion and garlic, season with salt, and cook until the onion is translucent. Set ¾ cup of the corn kernels aside and add the rest to the pan. Add 2 cups of the cream and cook until the corn is very tender, about 15 to 20 minutes.

4   Strain, reserve the cream, and transfer the solids to the blender. Puree until smooth, adding the cream as needed if the mixture is too thick. Season to taste and allow the puree to cool completely.

5   Place the flour, cornmeal, 2½ tablespoons of salt, brown sugar, baking powder, cayenne pepper, and paprika in a large mixing bowl and stir until combined. Place 2 cups of the corn puree, the honey, eggs, remaining cream, and sour cream in a separate large mixing bowl and stir until combined. Gradually add the dry mixture to the wet mixture and whisk to combine. When all of the dry mixture has been incorporated, add the reserved corn kernels and fold the mixture until they are evenly distributed.

6   Grease an 11 x 7-inch baking pan and pour the batter into it. Place the pan in the oven and bake until a toothpick inserted into the center comes out clean, about 35 minutes. Remove from the oven and briefly cool before cutting.

SUMMER VEGETABLE CHEESE DIP

THIS VERSATILE DIP is a go-to recipe for us. Its ability to accommodate leafy greens, slices of crusty bread, and almost any vegetable allows us to deploy it at farms all over New England.—*K.S.*

YIELD: 4 TO 6 SERVINGS ⟶ **ACTIVE TIME: 20 MINUTES** ⟶ **TOTAL TIME: 1 HOUR AND 45 MINUTES**

1 cup cream cheese or quark

½ cup sour cream

1 cup shredded mozzarella, plus more for topping

2 tablespoons fresh rosemary leaves

2 tablespoons fresh thyme leaves

½ cup diced summer squash

1 cup Swiss chard

1 cup spinach

6 garlic cloves, diced

2 teaspoons salt

1 teaspoon pepper

Slices of crusty bread, for serving

1 Place the cream cheese or quark, sour cream, and mozzarella in a bowl and stir until well combined.

2 Add the remaining ingredients for the dip, stir to combine, and place in the refrigerator for at least 1 hour.

3 Approximately 30 minutes before you are ready to serve the dip, preheat the oven to 350°F.

4 Transfer the dip to an oven-safe bowl, top with additional mozzarella, and bake until the cheese is melted and starting to brown, about 20 minutes. Remove from the oven and serve warm with slices of crusty bread.

NOTE: Quark is a creamy, unripe cheese that is popular in Germany and eastern European countries. If you're intrigued, check out your local dairy farm.

ZUCCHINI FRITTERS WITH SUMAC YOGURT

ZUCCHINI HAS A NUMBER of wonderful uses, and turning it into fritters is one of the easiest ways to get people excited about this summer squash. We spend so much time on farms that there are always plenty of opportunities to forage. Staghorn sumac is prevalent in New England, but its citric quality is massively underutilized (outside of Middle Eastern cuisine). By grinding it into a powder and using it as an accent here, Chris and I intend on remedying that oversight.—*K.S.*

YIELD: 4 SERVINGS ⋯⊷ **ACTIVE TIME: 15 MINUTES** ⋯⊷ **TOTAL TIME: 30 MINUTES**

1½ lbs. zucchini

¼ cup all-purpose flour

¼ cup grated Parmesan cheese

1 egg, beaten

3 tablespoons canola oil

1 cup yogurt

2 teaspoons fresh lemon juice

2 tablespoons sumac powder

Salt and pepper, to taste

1 Grate the zucchini into a large bowl. Line a colander with cheesecloth and then place the pieces in the colander, salt them, and let stand for 1 hour. Then press down to remove as much water from the zucchini as you can.

2 Place the zucchini, flour, Parmesan, and egg in a mixing bowl and stir to combine.

3 Use your hands to form handfuls of the mixture into balls and then gently press down on the balls to form them into patties.

4 Place the canola oil in a cast-iron skillet and warm over medium-high heat.

5 Working in batches, place the patties into the oil, taking care not to crowd the skillet. Cook until golden brown, about 5 minutes. Flip them over and cook for another 5 minutes, until the fritters are also golden brown on that side. Remove from the skillet and drain on a paper towel–lined plate.

6 Place the yogurt, lemon juice, and sumac powder in a small bowl and stir to combine.

7 Season the fritters with salt and pepper and serve the yogurt on the side.

PORK PÂTÉ (AKA GORTON)

ONCE I GAINED MY FOOTING AS A CHEF, I found myself continually revisiting the dishes that inspired me growing up. This French-Canadian delicacy is one, and it holds a very special place in my life, as my grandmother made it for every holiday. I hope that when you make my version, you can feel the love she put into it. —*K.S.*

YIELD: 10 TO 15 SERVINGS ⟶ **ACTIVE TIME: 20 MINUTES** ⟶ **TOTAL TIME: 24 HOURS**

3- to 5-lb., bone-in pork shoulder

3 onions, sliced

2 teaspoons ground cloves

1 tablespoon salt, plus more to taste

4 bay leaves

2 teaspoons black pepper, plus more to taste

1 teaspoon nutmeg

1 Preheat the oven to 300°F.

2 Place all of the ingredients in a Dutch oven and stir to combine. Cover, and cook over low heat until the pork falls apart at the touch of a fork, about 3 to 4 hours.

3 Remove from heat, discard the bay leaves, and transfer the pork shoulder to a plate. When the pork shoulder has cooled slightly, shred it with a fork.

4 Place the shredded pork and ½ cup of the juices from the pot in a blender. Puree until it forms a paste, adding more of the juices as needed.

5 Season with salt and pepper, transfer the paste to a large jar, and then pour the remaining juices over it. Cover the jar and store it in the refrigerator overnight before serving.

SUMMER SALAD WITH OREGANO VINAIGRETTE

ONCE TOMATO SEASON IS IN FULL SWING, things become a lot easier for chefs in New England. As this stripped-down salad shows, when you've got an ingredient as good as fresh heirloom tomatoes, you do all you can to stay out of its way.—*C.V.*

YIELD: 4 TO 6 SERVINGS ⟶ **ACTIVE TIME: 10 MINUTES** ⟶ **TOTAL TIME: 20 MINUTES**

FOR THE VINAIGRETTE

¼ cup champagne vinegar

½ shallot

1 teaspoon Dijon mustard

2 tablespoons honey

1 teaspoon salt

¼ teaspoon black pepper

2 ice cubes

¾ cup vegetable oil

1 tablespoon chopped oregano

FOR THE SALAD

3 heads of romaine lettuce, chopped

2 heirloom tomatoes, diced

1 cucumber, diced

Salt and pepper, to taste

Shaved Parmesan cheese, for garnish

1 Prepare the vinaigrette. Place all of the ingredients, except for the oil and oregano, in a blender. Puree, starting on low speed and increasing to high, and add the oil in a slow stream.

2 When the mixture is emulsified, transfer to a mixing bowl, add the oregano, and stir to incorporate. Season to taste and set aside.

3 Place the lettuce, tomatoes, and cucumber in a large mixing bowl. Season with salt and pepper and add ½ cup of the vinaigrette. Toss to combine, taste, and season with more of the vinaigrette, if desired. Plate and garnish with the shaved Parmesan.

NOTE: You may be confused by the inclusion of the ice cubes in the vinaigrette, but it is necessary to ensure that the mixture does not get too warm in the blender, which would prevent it from emulsifying.

PANZANELLA WITH WHITE BALSAMIC VINAIGRETTE

DURING THE BUSY NEW ENGLAND SUMMER, the best-laid plans for a quiet night at home are often waylaid, making quick dishes that can salvage ingredients which have lingered slightly too long, extremely valuable. This salad is one such treasure, sprucing up day-old bread and soft, overripe heirloom tomatoes.—*C.V.*

YIELD: 4 TO 6 SERVINGS ⇢ **ACTIVE TIME: 25 MINUTES** ⇢ **TOTAL TIME: 45 MINUTES**

FOR THE SALAD

1 tablespoon salt, plus 2 teaspoons

½ cup pearl onions, trimmed

Kernels from 1 ear of corn

1 cup green beans, cut into bite-sized pieces

4 cups cubed day-old bread

2 cups chopped overripe tomatoes

10 large basil leaves, torn

Cracked black pepper, to taste

FOR THE VINAIGRETTE

½ cup white balsamic vinegar

¼ cup vegetable oil

2 tablespoons minced shallot

4 tablespoons sliced scallions

2 tablespoons chopped parsley leaves

2 teaspoons salt

1 teaspoon black pepper

1 Bring water to a boil in a small saucepan and prepare an ice water bath in a mixing bowl.

2 When the water is boiling, add the 1 tablespoon of salt and the pearl onions and cook for 5 minutes. When the onions have 1 minute left to cook, add the corn and green beans to the saucepan and cook for 1 minute. Transfer the vegetables to the water bath and let cool completely.

3 Remove the pearl onions from the water bath and squeeze to remove the bulbs from their skins. Cut the bulbs in half and break them down into individual petals. Drain the corn and green beans and pat dry.

4 Prepare the vinaigrette. Place all of the ingredients in a mixing bowl and whisk until combined.

5 Place the cooked vegetables, bread, tomatoes, and basil in a salad bowl and toss to combine. Add the remaining salt, season with pepper, and add half of the vinaigrette. Toss to evenly coat, taste, and add more of the vinaigrette if desired.

WATERMELON SALAD WITH RICOTTA & ARUGULA

THIS LIGHT SALAD IS THE PERFECT WAY to keep a hot day from getting the better of you. Pitting the spicy bite of arugula against creamy ricotta and the refreshing sweetness of watermelon will keep you in the right state of mind: ready to celebrate the brief glory that is summer in New England.—*K.S.*

YIELD: 4 SERVINGS ⟶ **ACTIVE TIME: 10 MINUTES** ⟶ **TOTAL TIME: 15 MINUTES**

4 cups arugula

2 tablespoons olive oil

Flesh of 1 large watermelon, cubed

1 cup ricotta cheese

Fresh cracked black pepper, to taste

1 Place the arugula in a salad bowl. Add the olive oil and toss to combine.

2 Divide the watermelon between four bowls and top each of them with a generous scoop of ricotta.

3 Add the dressed arugula, season with the black pepper, and serve.

MELON, CUCUMBER & PROSCIUTTO SALAD
WITH MINT VINAIGRETTE

THE VERSATILE MELON CAN comfortably straddle the sweet-and-savory divide. Here it cozies up beside crispy, cured prosciutto and creamy feta to carry this dynamic salad. —*CV*

YIELD: 4 TO 6 SERVINGS ⟶ **ACTIVE TIME: 15 MINUTES** ⟶ **TOTAL TIME: 45 MINUTES**

FOR THE SALAD

8 slices of prosciutto

3 cups diced cantaloupe

3 cups diced honeydew melon

2 cups sliced cucumber

Salt and pepper, to taste

1 jalapeño pepper, sliced

⅔ cup feta cheese

Mint leaves, chopped, for garnish

FOR THE VINAIGRETTE

3 tablespoons chopped mint

¼ cup olive oil

3 tablespoons apple cider vinegar

1 tablespoon honey

2 teaspoons diced shallot

1 teaspoon salt

¼ teaspoon pepper

1   Preheat the oven to 350°F.

2   Place the prosciutto on a parchment–lined baking sheet. Cover with another sheet of parchment and place another baking sheet that is the same size on top. Place in the oven and bake until the prosciutto is crisp, about 12 minutes. Remove from the oven and let cool. When the prosciutto is cool enough to handle, chop it into bite-sized pieces.

3   Prepare the vinaigrette. Place all of the ingredients in a mixing bowl and whisk until thoroughly combined. Set aside.

4   Place the cantaloupe, honeydew melon, and cucumber in a salad bowl, season with salt and pepper, and toss to combine. Add the jalapeño and vinaigrette and toss until evenly coated. Plate the salad, top with the chopped prosciutto and feta, and garnish with mint leaves.

SHAVED SQUASH SALAD WITH HERB VINAIGRETTE

THIS SALAD IS THE COUSIN OF A DISH I CAME UP WITH during a cooking competition where I was given various squashes and a number of other heavy items. By keeping it simple—shaving the vegetables and seasoning them with a light dressing—I was able to achieve some balance and win kudos from the judges.—*C.V.*

YIELD: 4 TO 6 SERVINGS ⟶ **ACTIVE TIME: 15 MINUTES** ⟶ **TOTAL TIME: 1 HOUR**

FOR THE SALAD

1 pint heirloom cherry tomatoes

1 tablespoon olive oil

5 garlic cloves, crushed

Leaves from 2 sprigs of thyme

½ teaspoon salt, plus more to taste

¼ teaspoon pepper, plus more to taste

3 zucchini, sliced thin with a mandoline

2 summer squash, sliced thin with a mandoline

1 red bell pepper, seeded and sliced thin with a mandoline

FOR THE VINAIGRETTE

1 tablespoon sliced chives

1 teaspoon chopped thyme

1 teaspoon chopped oregano

1 tablespoon chopped parsley

3 tablespoons apple cider vinegar

1 tablespoon honey

2 teaspoons diced shallot

1 teaspoon salt

¼ teaspoon pepper

¼ cup olive oil

1   Preheat the broiler to high. Place the cherry tomatoes, olive oil, garlic, thyme, salt, and pepper in a mixing bowl and toss until the tomatoes are evenly coated. Place the tomatoes on a baking sheet, place in the oven, and broil until the skins begin to burst, 6 to 8 minutes. Remove from the oven and let cool completely.

2   Prepare the vinaigrette. Place all of the ingredients, except for the olive oil, in a mixing bowl and whisk to combine. Add the oil in a slow stream while whisking to incorporate. Season to taste and set aside.

3   Place the zucchini, squash, and pepper in a large mixing bowl, season with salt and pepper, and add the vinaigrette. Toss to evenly coat, plate the salad, and sprinkle the blistered tomatoes over the top.

CHILLED CORN SALAD

THIS RECIPE, WHICH IS A RIFF on a classic Mexican dish known as *esquites*, is a staple at both my house and The Farmers Dinner, albeit altered slightly to facilitate the rapidly shifting seasons. —*K.S.*

YIELD: 4 TO 6 SERVINGS — **ACTIVE TIME: 15 MINUTES** — **TOTAL TIME: 4 TO 24 HOURS**

2 cups corn kernels
(about 5 ears of corn)

2 tablespoons unsalted butter

1 jalapeño pepper, seeded and diced
(add more if you like things spicy)

½ teaspoon salt

2 tablespoons mayonnaise

2 teaspoons garlic powder

3 tablespoons sour cream or Mexican crema

¼ teaspoon cayenne pepper

¼ teaspoon chili powder

2 tablespoons feta cheese

2 tablespoons Cotija cheese

2 teaspoons fresh lime juice

½ cup cilantro, chopped

Salt and pepper, to taste

1 Preheat the oven to 400°F.

2 Place the corn on a baking sheet and bake in the oven until it turns a light golden brown, about 35 minutes.

3 Remove the corn from the oven, let cool slightly, and then transfer to a large mixing bowl. Add the remaining ingredients and stir to combine.

4 Place the salad in the refrigerator for at least 3 hours, although letting it chill overnight is highly recommended.

NOTE: The amount of jalapeño suggested in the ingredients is a safe amount of heat to serve to a broad spectrum of tastes. If you and yours like things spicier, feel free to include the seeds or another jalapeño.

GRILLED CORN WITH
CHIPOTLE MAYONNAISE & GOAT CHEESE

DURING ONE OF MY trips to Mexico I was introduced to *elotes*, more commonly known as Mexican street corn. Every summer, as soon as locally grown corn hits the market, I recreate this dish as many times as possible. It's got it all—sweet corn, spice from the chipotle, and a soft, creamy landing thanks to the goat cheese.—*C.V.*

YIELD: 6 SERVINGS ⋯► **ACTIVE TIME: 25 MINUTES** ⋯► **TOTAL TIME: 1 HOUR AND 15 MINUTES**

6 ears of corn

3 chipotle peppers in adobo

½ cup mayonnaise

¼ cup sour cream

1½ tablespoons brown sugar

1 tablespoon fresh lime juice

2 tablespoons chopped cilantro, plus more for garnish

1 teaspoon salt, plus more to taste

½ teaspoon black pepper, plus more to taste

3 tablespoons olive oil

½ cup crumbled goat cheese

6 lime wedges, for serving

1 Preheat the oven to 400°F.

2 Place the ears of corn on a baking sheet, place it in the oven, and bake for 25 minutes, until the kernels have a slight give to them. Remove from the oven and let cool. When the ears of corn are cool enough to handle, remove the husks and silk.

3 Preheat your gas or charcoal grill to 400°F. Place the chipotles, mayonnaise, sour cream, brown sugar, lime juice, cilantro, salt, and pepper in a food processor and puree until smooth. Set aside.

4 Drizzle the corn with olive oil, season with salt and pepper, and place on the grill. Cook, while turning, until they are charred all over.

5 Spread the mayonnaise on the corn, sprinkle the goat cheese on top, and garnish with additional cilantro. Serve with wedges of lime.

CHARRED BRASSICAS WITH PICKLED RAMPS & BUTTERMILK CAESAR DRESSING

BROCCOLI, BRUSSELS SPROUTS, AND CAULIFLOWER are but a few of the fine members of the brassica family. Charring them brings out their sweet side, which pairs wonderfully with the creamy and slightly acidic buttermilk dressing.—*C.V.*

YIELD: 4 TO 6 SERVINGS ⋯•⋯ **ACTIVE TIME: 20 MINUTES** ⋯•⋯ **TOTAL TIME: 45 MINUTES**

1 large garlic clove, minced

2 anchovy fillets

⅔ cup mayonnaise

¼ cup buttermilk

¼ cup grated Parmesan cheese, plus more for garnish

Zest of 1 lemon

1 teaspoon Worcestershire sauce

1 teaspoon salt, plus more to taste

½ teaspoon black pepper, plus more to taste

1 small head of cauliflower, cut into bite-sized pieces

1 head of broccoli, cut into florets

¼ cup canola oil

¼ lb. Brussels sprouts, trimmed and halved

10 to 12 Pickled Ramps (see page 189)

Red pepper flakes, for garnish

1 Place the garlic, anchovies, mayonnaise, buttermilk, Parmesan, lemon zest, Worcestershire sauce, salt, and pepper in a food processor and puree until combined. Season to taste and set the dressing aside.

2 Bring a large pot of salted water to a boil. Add the cauliflower, cook for 1 minute, remove with a slotted spoon, and transfer to a paper towel–lined plate. Wait for the water to return to a boil, add the broccoli, and cook for 30 seconds. Use a slotted spoon to remove the broccoli and let the water drip off before transferring it to the paper towel–lined plate.

3 Place the canola oil and Brussels sprouts, cut side down, in a large cast-iron skillet. Add the broccoli and cauliflower, season with salt and pepper, and cook over high heat without moving the vegetables. Cook until charred, turn over, and cook until charred on that side. Remove and transfer to a bowl.

4 Add the Pickled Ramps and dressing to the bowl and toss to evenly coat. Garnish with additional Parmesan and red pepper flakes and serve.

GARLIC & CHILI BROCCOLINI

THE SPICY BROCCOLI AT ONE OF MY FAVORITE SPOTS in Boston's Chinatown always makes the trip into the big city worthwhile. Thinking about it one day, I realized that the sweeter flavor of broccolini would be an even better match for all that spice, and came up with this lovely, simple side.—*C.V.*

YIELD: 4 SERVINGS ⟶ **ACTIVE TIME: 10 MINUTES** ⟶ **TOTAL TIME: 30 MINUTES**

Salt and pepper, to taste

½ lb. broccolini, ends trimmed

4 tablespoons olive oil

1 tablespoon minced garlic

1 teaspoon red pepper flakes

2 tablespoons toasted almonds, for garnish

1   Bring a large pot of salted water to a boil. Add the broccolini and cook for 30 seconds. Remove with a strainer, allow the majority of the water to drip off, and transfer to a paper towel–lined plate.

2   Place the olive oil in a large sauté pan and warm over medium-high heat.

3   When the oil starts to smoke, add the broccolini and cook until well browned. Turn the broccolini over, add the garlic, season with salt and pepper, and toss to combine. When the broccolini is browned all over, add the red pepper flakes and toss to evenly distribute.

4   Transfer to a serving platter and garnish with the toasted almonds.

NEW POTATO SALAD

THE SWEETNESS OF NEW POTATOES amid a medley of fresh, flavorful veggies makes this dish my favorite place to turn when I need a potato fix in the early summer. Break this out at your next barbecue and your days of boiled potatoes drenched in mayo are long past.—*E.V.*

YIELD: 4 TO 6 SERVINGS ··•· **ACTIVE TIME: 30 MINUTES** ··•· **TOTAL TIME: 2 HOURS AND 30 MINUTES**

1 bulb of garlic

3 tablespoons olive oil

Salt and pepper, to taste

1 lb. new potatoes, halved

½ lb. green beans, trimmed and chopped

10 pearl onions, trimmed

2 cups arugula

2 teaspoons red wine vinegar

1 Preheat the oven to 400°F.

2 Remove the loose papery skin from the bulb of garlic and cut off the top so that all of the cloves are exposed. Shape a piece of aluminum foil into a pouch, place the garlic into it, and drizzle with 1 tablespoon of the olive oil. Sprinkle with salt, seal the pouch, and place it in a baking dish. Place the dish in the oven and bake for 35 to 40 minutes, until the cloves of garlic are golden brown.

3 Remove from the oven, remove the garlic from the pouch, and reserve the oil. Keep the oven at 400°F. When the garlic is cool enough to handle, squeeze the bottom of the garlic bulb to extract the roasted cloves. Transfer them to a small bowl, mash with a fork, and place in a small container.

4 Place the potatoes on a baking sheet, season with salt and pepper, and drizzle with the remaining 2 tablespoons of olive oil. Place the potatoes in the oven and roast until fork tender, about 30 to 35 minutes. Remove from the oven and let cool completely.

5 Bring a pot of salted water to a boil and prepare an ice water bath in a medium bowl. When the water starts to boil, add the green beans and cook for 1 minute. Remove with a slotted spoon and transfer to the ice water bath.

6 When the pot of water comes back to a boil, add the pearl onions and cook until tender, about 5 minutes. While the onions are cooking, remove the green beans from the ice water bath, pat dry, and transfer to a mixing bowl. Remove the onions from the water with a slotted spoon and place them in the ice water bath until they have cooled completely. Squeeze to remove the bulbs from their peels, halve, and break each onion down into individual petals.

7 Add the roasted new potatoes, pearl onion petals, arugula, 2 teaspoons of the mashed roasted garlic, the reserved olive oil, and the red wine vinegar to the mixing bowl containing the green beans. Season with salt and pepper, toss to evenly coat, and serve.

NEW ENGLAND LOBSTER ROLLS
WITH BROWNED BUTTER–MILK CRUMBS

SUMMER MEANS SEAFOOD IN NEW ENGLAND, and no transformation of the ocean's bounty is more iconic than the lobster roll. This classic traditionally comes in one of two styles—either with mayonnaise or browned butter—and this recipe provides the best of both worlds.—*K.S.*

YIELD: 2 TO 4 SERVINGS ⋯ **ACTIVE TIME: 10 MINUTES** ⋯ **TOTAL TIME: 25 MINUTES**

1 stick of unsalted butter

1 cup nonfat milk powder

2 to 4 buns

Meat from 2 to 3 cooked chicken lobsters

2 tablespoons mayonnaise

Salt and pepper, to taste

1 Place the butter in a small saucepan and melt it over low heat.

2 When the butter is melted, stir in the milk powder and cook until the mixture starts to turn golden brown.

3 Remove the pan from heat and strain through a fine sieve over a bowl. Store the crumbs in an airtight container and reserve the browned butter.

4 Place the buns in a skillet with the reserved browned butter and cook for 1 minute on each side, until golden brown. Remove and set aside.

5 Place the lobster meat, mayonnaise, salt, and pepper in a mixing bowl and stir to combine.

6 Spoon the dressed lobster into the toasted buns, top with a generous amount of the browned butter-milk crumbs, and serve.

LOBSTER TOSTADAS WITH CHARRED CORN SALSA & CILANTRO–LIME SOUR CREAM

FOR ME, TACOS ARE NOT LIMITED TO TUESDAYS. In my opinion, a taco is one of the most versatile tools in a chef's arsenal, able to incorporate an unthinkable amount of ingredients and still shine. Lobster and corn are natural partners, but charring the corn adds a bit of a depth and mystery to this dish. —*C.V.*

YIELD: 4 SERVINGS ···• **ACTIVE TIME: 20 MINUTES** ···• **TOTAL TIME: 1 HOUR AND 30 MINUTES**

FOR THE TOSTADAS & SALSA

2 ears of corn, husked, silk removed, and rinsed

1 tablespoon olive oil

Salt and pepper, to taste

1 small jalapeño pepper, seeded and diced, plus more for garnish

¼ cup diced red onion

2 teaspoons minced garlic

1½ tablespoons fresh lime juice

¼ cup chopped cilantro, plus more for garnish

½ cup diced tomato

2 cups canola oil

8 corn tortillas

Paprika, to taste

Meat from 4 cooked chicken lobsters

Red cabbage, diced, for garnish

Lime wedges, for serving

FOR THE SOUR CREAM

½ cup chopped cilantro

¼ cup fresh lime juice

1¼ cups sour cream

1½ teaspoons salt

½ teaspoon black pepper

1 Preheat your gas or charcoal grill to 400°F.

2 Drizzle the corn with the olive oil, season with salt and pepper, and place them on the grill. Cook, while turning, until they are charred all over. Remove from the grill and let cool.

3 When the corn is cool enough to handle, remove the kernels and place them in a mixing bowl. Add the jalapeño, onion, garlic, lime juice, cilantro, and tomato and stir to combine.

4 Prepare the sour cream. Place all of the ingredients in a mixing bowl, stir to combine, and set aside.

5 Place the canola oil in a Dutch oven and warm to 350°F over medium-high heat. Working with one tortilla at a time, place them into the oil and fry until golden brown. Remove from the oil, transfer to a paper towel–lined plate, and season with salt and paprika.

6 Spread some of the sour cream on each tortilla and top with the salsa and lobster meat. Garnish with jalapeño, cilantro, and red cabbage and serve with lime wedges.

ROASTED CORN & RED PEPPER BISQUE
WITH BUTTER-POACHED LOBSTER

DURING THE DOG DAYS OF SUMMER IN NEW ENGLAND, you can find corn almost everywhere, and its sweetness is a perfect match for the famously fresh taste of Maine lobster. This dish proves what I always tell young chefs in New England: we are spoiled by all of the great ingredients that the region makes available.—*K.S.*

YIELD: 4 SERVINGS → **ACTIVE TIME: 30 MINUTES** → **TOTAL TIME: 50 MINUTES**

3 cups fresh corn kernels (about 7 ears of corn)

2 tablespoons vegetable oil

Salt and pepper, to taste

3 red bell peppers

1½ sticks of unsalted butter

½ cup heavy cream

½ cup milk

Meat from 2 cooked chicken lobsters

1 Preheat the oven to 375°F.

2 Place the corn in a single layer on a large baking sheet and drizzle with the vegetable oil. Season with salt, place in the oven, and bake until the corn starts to darken and caramelize, 12 to 18 minutes. Remove from the oven and raise the temperature to 425°F.

3 Place the peppers on a baking sheet and place them in the oven. Cook, while turning occasionally, until the skin is blistered all over, about 30 minutes. Remove from the oven and let cool. When cool enough to handle, remove the skins and seeds and discard. Set the peppers aside.

4 Place the corn, peppers, ½ stick of butter, cream, and milk in a saucepan and bring to a simmer, while stirring, over medium heat. Simmer for 20 minutes, making sure that it does not come to a boil.

5 While the bisque is simmering, place the remaining butter in a small saucepan and melt over low heat. Add the lobster meat and cook for 7 to 10 minutes, spooning the butter over the lobster as it cooks. When the lobster is tender and warmed through, remove from heat and set aside.

6 After simmering for 20 minutes, remove the bisque from heat and let cool for 10 minutes.

7 Transfer the bisque to a blender and puree until smooth. If the mixture has cooled too much, return to the saucepan and cook until warmed through. If not, ladle into warmed bowls and top each one with pieces of the poached lobster.

BLACKENING SPICE

YIELD: ¼ CUP
ACTIVE TIME: 5 MINUTES
TOTAL TIME: 5 MINUTES

1 ½ tablespoons paprika

1 tablespoon chili powder

1 tablespoon cumin

½ tablespoon ground coriander seeds

½ teaspoon cayenne pepper

1 tablespoon onion powder

2 teaspoons garlic powder

2 teaspoons black pepper

Place all of the ingredients in a mixing bowl and stir to combine.

BLACKENED SALMON
WITH GRILLED VEGETABLE SALAD

DURING THE SUMMER, Keith and I are always pressed to find lighter dishes that are still hearty enough to serve as an entrée. This dish has that rare balance, as salmon is a fattier fish with deep flavor, and the vegetables keep everyone light on their feet.—*C.V.*

YIELD: 6 SERVINGS → **ACTIVE TIME: 25 MINUTES** → **TOTAL TIME: 24 HOURS**

½ cup dried cannellini beans, soaked overnight

1 tablespoon minced garlic

2 teaspoons chopped thyme

2 teaspoons chopped oregano

1 teaspoon black pepper

3 teaspoons salt, plus more to taste

11 tablespoons olive oil

1 zucchini, cut into ½-inch pieces

1 small eggplant, cut into ½-inch pieces

2 red bell peppers, seeded and cut into ½-inch pieces

6 oz. arugula

2 tablespoons red wine vinegar

2 teaspoons honey

2 tablespoons canola oil

6 (6 oz.) pieces of skinless salmon

¼ cup Blackening Spice (see sidebar)

Zest of 1 lemon

6 lemon wedges, for serving

1 Drain the beans, place them in a saucepan, and cover with water. Cook over medium heat until tender, about 50 minutes, drain, and set aside.

2 Place the garlic, thyme, oregano, pepper, 2 teaspoons of the salt, and 8 tablespoons of the olive oil in a mixing bowl and whisk until combined.

3 Preheat your gas or charcoal grill to 400°F. Place the zucchini, eggplant, and bell peppers in a baking dish, cover with the olive oil mixture, and let sit for 20 minutes. Preheat the oven to 450°F.

4 Place the vegetables on the grill and cook, while turning often, until cooked through. Transfer to a cutting board, let cool, and then cut into bite-sized pieces.

5 Place the vegetables in a large mixing bowl with the arugula, vinegar, honey, cooked beans, remaining salt, and remaining olive oil. Toss to evenly coat and set aside.

6 Place the canola oil in a large cast-iron skillet and warm over medium-high heat. Season the salmon with salt and the Blackening Spice. When the oil starts to smoke, carefully place the salmon in the skillet and then transfer it to the oven. Cook until the internal temperature of each piece is 135°F, about 3 to 4 minutes. Remove from the oven and sprinkle each piece with lemon zest. Serve over the salad with a lemon wedge on the side.

CORNMEAL–CRUSTED POLLOCK
WITH ROSEMARY CHIPS

THIS DISH IS AN HOMAGE TO CAPTAIN TIM of the F/V Finlander, and all of New England's fishmongers. For it is only through their hard work that Chris and I came to fall in love with pollock.—*K.S.*

YIELD: 2 TO 4 SERVINGS ➝ **ACTIVE TIME: 20 MINUTES** ➝ **TOTAL TIME: 45 MINUTES**

4 cups canola oil

5 potatoes, sliced into long, thin strips

3 tablespoons minced fresh rosemary leaves

Salt and pepper, to taste

2 eggs, beaten

1 cup cornmeal

1 to 1½ lbs. pollock fillets

1 Place the canola oil in a Dutch oven and bring to 350°F over medium-high heat.

2 When the oil is ready, place the sliced potatoes in the oil and cook until golden brown. Remove and set to drain on a paper towel–lined plate. Keep the oil at 350°F.

3 When drained to your liking, place the fried potatoes in a bowl with the rosemary and salt and toss to coat. Set aside.

4 Place the beaten eggs in a small bowl and the cornmeal in another. Dip the pollock fillets into the egg and then into the cornmeal, repeating until coated all over.

5 Place the battered pollock in the oil and cook until golden brown. Remove and set to drain on another paper towel–lined plate. Serve with the rosemary chips.

FOR THE STEW

18 littleneck clams

1 tablespoon salt, plus more to taste

6 tablespoons olive oil

1 eggplant, diced

1 zucchini, diced

1 summer squash, diced

2 red bell peppers, diced

Black pepper, to taste

¼ cup diced shallot

2 tablespoons diced garlic

1 cup white wine

½ lb. mussels, cleaned and debearded (see page 188)

4 cups Tomato Sauce (see page 198)

½ lb. small shrimp, peeled and deveined

1 tablespoon fresh lemon juice

2 tablespoons chopped parsley, plus more for garnish

6 (5 oz.) pieces of pollock

Lemon wedges, for serving

FOR THE POLENTA

6 tablespoons butter

1 cup diced onion

6 cups water

1 cup coarse cornmeal

1 tablespoon salt

NEW ENGLAND SEAFOOD STEW
WITH CREAMY POLENTA

ONE SUMMER I HAD THE PRIVILEGE of taking a deep-sea fishing trip with New England fishmongers. The boat was strictly rod-and-reel, meaning no fishing nets or other contraptions. Still, their tireless efforts resulted in an incredible haul, and this stew is a tip of the hat to those hardworking individuals who ferry the gifts of the sea back to shore.—*C.V.*

YIELD: 6 SERVINGS ⋯ **ACTIVE TIME: 1 HOUR** ⋯ **TOTAL TIME: 3 HOURS AND 45 MINUTES**

1 Place the clams and salt in a bowl and cover with cold water. Soak for 2 hours to remove some of the sand, changing the water every 30 minutes.

2 Place half of the olive oil in a large sauté pan and warm over medium-high heat. When the oil starts to smoke, place the eggplant, zucchini, squash, and peppers in the pan and cook until almost tender, about 6 minutes. Season with salt and pepper, add the shallot and garlic, and cook for another minute. Remove from heat and set aside.

3 Prepare the polenta. Place the butter in a saucepan and melt over medium heat. Add the onion and cook until translucent. Add the water and bring to a boil. Gradually add the cornmeal, whisking constantly to prevent lumps from forming. When all of the cornmeal has been incorporated, reduce the heat to low and cook, while stirring frequently, until the cornmeal is tender. Add the salt, remove from heat, and set aside.

4 Preheat the oven to 450°F. Drain the clams and place them in a large saucepan. Add the wine, cover, and cook over high heat until the majority of the clams are starting to open, about 8 minutes. Add the mussels and sauce, cover, and cook until the majority of the mussels have opened. Discard any clams and mussels that have not opened. Add the shrimp and cooked vegetables, stir to combine, and cook until everything is heated through. Add the lemon juice, 2 tablespoons of olive oil, and parsley, season with salt and pepper, and remove from heat.

5 Place the remaining olive oil in a cast-iron skillet and warm over high heat. Season the pollock with salt and pepper, place in the pan, and cook until golden brown. Flip the pieces over, place the skillet in the oven, and cook until the fish is cooked through, about 4 minutes.

6 To serve, spoon some of the polenta into a bowl and place a piece of pollock on top. Surround with the shellfish and vegetables and ladle some of the broth into each bowl. Garnish with additional parsley and serve with lemon wedges.

SEARED SCALLOP & SWEET CORN CHOWDER

IT'S HARD NOT TO FEEL BLESSED after tasting fresh corn and scallops and realizing that not everyone has them on their doorstep. If you or a loved one starts taking the wonders available in New England for granted, prepare this chowder for them. It's sweet, but setting that off with some smoked paprika and chili oil makes for a memorable bowl.—*K.S.*

YIELD: 6 SERVINGS ⟶ **ACTIVE TIME: 35 MINUTES** ⟶ **TOTAL TIME: 1 HOUR AND 15 MINUTES**

6 tablespoons unsalted butter

1 large onion, diced

6 strips of bacon, cooked and diced

2 celery stalks, chopped

2 garlic cloves, minced

¼ cup all-purpose flour

3 cups fresh corn kernels (about 7 ears of corn)

3 sprigs of thyme

2 large potatoes, diced

½ cup heavy cream

½ cup whole milk

Salt and pepper, to taste

1 tablespoon olive oil

6 fresh scallops

1 Place the butter in a large skillet and cook over medium heat until it is melted. Add the onion and sauté until it starts to turn golden brown.

2 Add the bacon, celery, and garlic and cook, while stirring frequently, for 5 minutes.

3 Add the flour and stir to ensure that the mixture is well combined.

4 Add the corn, thyme, potatoes, cream, and milk, stir to combine, and bring to a simmer. Season with salt and pepper and cook until the potatoes are fork tender.

5 Place a tablespoon of olive oil in another skillet and warm over medium-high heat.

6 Pat the scallops dry and season with salt. When the oil is hot, place the scallops in and cook for about 2 to 3 minutes on each side, until golden brown.

7 Remove the sprigs of thyme from the soup and discard. Ladle the soup into warmed bowls and top each bowl with 1 scallop.

OYSTER SLIDERS WITH RED PEPPER MAYONNAISE

THE BRINY TASTE OF oysters always brings me back to fond memories of summers spent on the Cape. This particular dish is a nod to my friend Patrick, who has helped out with several Farmers Dinners. At one event, he created a fried oyster slider with preserved lemon on a squid ink bun. He tested the buns many times to get them right, and later we joked that King's Hawaiian Rolls would be nearly as tasty. We both laughed, but fried oysters are good enough that it turned out to be true.—*K.S.*

YIELD: 4 SERVINGS ···► **ACTIVE TIME: 30 MINUTES** ···► **TOTAL TIME: 1 HOUR AND 15 MINUTES**

3 red bell peppers

1 cup canola oil

1 cup cornmeal

Salt, to taste

½ lb. oyster meat

2 eggs, beaten

1 tablespoon unsalted butter

4 King's Hawaiian Rolls

½ cup mayonnaise

1 Preheat the oven to 400°F.

2 Place the red peppers on a baking sheet and bake, while turning occasionally, for 35 to 40 minutes, until they are blistered all over. Remove from the oven and let cool. When cool enough to handle, remove the skins and seeds and set the flesh aside.

3 Place the oil in a Dutch oven and bring it to 350°F over medium-high heat.

4 Place the cornmeal and salt in a bowl and stir to combine.

5 When the oil is ready, dip the oyster meat into the beaten eggs and the cornmeal-and-salt mixture. Repeat until evenly coated.

6 Place the oysters in the Dutch oven and fry until golden brown, about 3 to 5 minutes. Remove from the oil and set on a paper towel–lined plate to drain.

7 Place the butter in a skillet and melt over medium heat. Place the buns in the skillet and toast until lightly browned. Remove and set aside.

8 Place the roasted peppers and mayonnaise in a blender and puree until smooth. Spread the red pepper mayonnaise on the buns, add the fried oysters, and serve.

BRAISED PORK BELLY WITH
TOASTED FARRO, CORN & SNAP PEAS

WHENEVER YOU MENTION PORK BELLY, you get a group of people saying, "I don't like it . . . there's too much fat." While it is true that the belly does have a high-fat content, it will render off if cooked properly, leaving a delicious, tender piece of meat. —*C.V.*

YIELD: 4 TO 6 SERVINGS ⋯► **ACTIVE TIME: 1 HOUR AND 30 MINUTES** ⋯► **TOTAL TIME: 24 HOURS**

1 The night before you're going to serve the preparation, preheat the oven to 350°F and place the farro on a baking sheet in an even layer. Place it in the oven and bake until it is a deep brown color. Remove from the oven, place it in a bowl, understanding that the grains will double in size, and cover with the water. Soak overnight.

2 Preheat the oven to 350°F. Place the ears of corn in the oven and cook until the kernels give slightly when squeezed. Remove from the oven and let cool. Lower the oven temperature to 250°F.

3 Place the pork belly skin side down and use a knife to score the flesh, slicing ⅛ inch deep in a diamond pattern. Season with salt and pepper and set aside.

4 Place the olive oil in a large Dutch oven and warm over high heat. When the oil starts to smoke, carefully place the pork belly, skin side down, in the pot to begin rendering the fat. Sear until the skin is brown, turn over, and sear until brown on the other side. Remove the pork belly from the pot and set aside.

5 Add the onions, carrots, celery, and garlic to the Dutch oven and cook until brown. Add 4 sprigs of thyme and the tomato paste, stir to coat the vegetables, and then add the wine. Scrape up any browned bits from the bottom of the Dutch oven and cook until the liquid starts to thicken. Add the stock, bring to a boil, and return the pork belly to the pot. Cover the Dutch oven and transfer it to the oven. Cook until the pork belly is tender, 2 to 2½ hours.

6 When the pork belly is tender, strain and reserve the liquid, discard the vegetables, set the pork belly aside, and place the liquid in a saucepan. Cook over high heat until it is thick and syrupy. Set aside.

7 Drain the farro and place it in a large pot with the water, shallot, 1 tablespoon salt, remaining thyme, and bay leaf. Bring to a boil over medium-high heat and then reduce the heat so that the mixture simmers. Cook until the farro is al dente, about 20 minutes. Remove, drain, and transfer to a bowl.

8 Remove the kernels from the roasted ears of corn. Bring a small pot of salted water to a boil, add the snap peas, and cook for 1 minute. Drain and add to the farro along with the corn, butter, and chives. Stir to combine, season with salt and pepper, and transfer to a serving dish.

9 Slice the pork belly and place on top of the farro-and-vegetable mixture. Spoon the reduced cooking liquid over the top and serve.

2 cups farro

3 ears of corn, husked, silk removed, and rinsed

4-lb., skin-on pork belly

1 tablespoon salt, plus more to taste

Pepper, to taste

2 tablespoons olive oil

2 large yellow onions, cut into 1-inch pieces

2 large carrots, cut into 1-inch pieces

4 celery stalks, cut into 1-inch pieces

6 garlic cloves, crushed

6 sprigs of thyme

3 tablespoons tomato paste

2 cups white wine

8 cups Chicken Stock (see page 236)

6 cups water

1 shallot, halved

1 bay leaf

4 oz. snap peas, trimmed and chopped

4 tablespoons unsalted butter

¼ cup sliced chives

BEEF & PORK BURGERS
WITH CARAMELIZED ONION MAYONNAISE

A GOOD BURGER IS HARD TO BEAT. This particular preparation is an homage to Miles Smith Farm in Loudon, New Hampshire, where they raise exquisite Scottish Highlander beef. A few years ago they started offering a mixture of ground beef and heritage pork that I quickly fell in love with, particularly when slathered in this sweet onion mayonnaise.—*K.S.*

YIELD: 6 SERVINGS ⋯ **ACTIVE TIME: 40 MINUTES** ⋯ **TOTAL TIME: 3 HOURS AND 30 MINUTES**

1 lb. ground beef

1 lb. ground pork

Salt and pepper, to taste

2 tablespoons unsalted butter

2 sweet onions, sliced thin

½ cup mayonnaise

6 brioche buns, toasted

6 slices of preferred cheese

1. Place the beef and pork in a mixing bowl and season with salt and pepper. Stir to combine, cover, and place in the refrigerator.

2. Place the butter in a skillet and melt over medium-low heat.

3. Add the onions and a pinch of salt and cook, while stirring frequently, until the onions develop a deep brown color, about 20 to 30 minutes. Remove from heat and let cool completely.

4. Transfer the cooled onions to a blender and puree until smooth. Place the puree and mayonnaise in a mixing bowl, season with salt and pepper, and stir to combine. Place the mixture in the refrigerator for at least 2 hours.

5. When ready to serve, preheat a grill to 450°F or place a cast-iron skillet over medium-high heat. Form the beef-and-pork mixture into 6 balls and then press down until they are patties.

6. Place the burgers on the grill or in the skillet and cook for 8 to 10 minutes. Flip the burgers over and cook until cooked through, about 5 to 8 minutes. If you're worried that they will dry out, don't fret. The pork fat will keep them moist and flavorful.

7. Spread the mayonnaise on one half of a bun. Place a burger on the other half of the bun, top each with a slice of cheese, and assemble.

APPLEWOOD-SMOKED RIBS
WITH MOLASSES BBQ SAUCE

NO ONE THINKS THAT "Yankees" know anything about barbecue. But unbelievable BBQ joints, like Ore Nell's in Kittery, Maine, and The Smoke Shop BBQ in Boston, are popping up all over New England. It's only a matter of time before these places put the region on the national BBQ map. The two recommendations here—for applewood and St. Louis-cut ribs—are not made lightly. Applewood is ideal because it is plentiful and adds amazing flavor to pork. The St. Louis cut—which removes the rib tips, sternum, and cartilage—ensures that the ribs cook evenly.—*K.S.*

YIELD: 10 SERVINGS ⇢ **ACTIVE TIME: 15 MINUTES** ⇢ **TOTAL TIME: 5 HOURS**

½ cup ketchup

¼ cup dark brown sugar

2 tablespoons granulated sugar

2 tablespoons Dijon mustard

3 tablespoons apple cider vinegar

2 garlic cloves, minced

¼ cup blackstrap molasses

¼ teaspoon ground cloves

½ teaspoon hot sauce

¼ cup honey

10 lbs. St. Louis-cut ribs

¼ cup salt

2 tablespoons light brown sugar

2 tablespoons garlic powder

1 tablespoon onion powder

1 tablespoon chili powder

1 tablespoon paprika

1 tablespoon cumin

2 cups applewood chips

8 cups apple juice or apple cider

1 Place the ketchup, dark brown sugar, granulated sugar, mustard, vinegar, garlic, molasses, cloves, hot sauce, and honey in a medium saucepan and bring to a boil over medium-high heat.

2 Reduce heat so that the sauce simmers and cook, while stirring occasionally, for 20 minutes. Remove pan from heat and set aside.

3 Place the ribs in a roasting pan. Place all of the remaining ingredients, except for the wood chips and the apple juice (or apple cider), in a bowl and stir until combined.

4 Rub the mixture in the bowl all over the ribs, making sure every inch is covered. Place the ribs in the refrigerator for 1 hour.

5 Heat your smoker to 250°F and place the sauce beside it. Once it reaches the desired temp, add the applewood chips and 1 cup of apple juice or cider to the steam tray. Place the ribs in the smoker and cook, while brushing the ribs with the sauce every 30 minutes, for about 4 hours, until the meat begins to shrink away from the bone. While the ribs are cooking, make sure you keep an eye on the steam tray and continue refilling it with apple juice or cider. You do not want the steam tray to be dry for any length of time.

6 When the ribs have finished cooking, remove from the smoker, wrap in foil, and try as hard as you can to let them rest for 20 minutes.

NOTE: If you do not have a smoker, you can still prepare this dish on your grill. Soak the applewood chips for 1 hour before grilling and either place them on the coals or, if using a gas grill, into a smoker box before placing the ribs on the grill.

6- to 8-lb., bone-in pork shoulder

Salt and pepper, to taste

1 large onion, diced

3 bay leaves

2 teaspoons paprika

¼ cup brown sugar

2 tablespoons peppercorns

7 cups Chicken Stock (see page 236)

1 tablespoon mustard

2 cups cornmeal

2 cups water

1 stick of unsalted butter

1 cup crumbled blue cheese

8 overripe peaches, pitted
and quartered

2 cups apple cider vinegar

¾ cup sugar

3 garlic cloves, chopped

6 jalapeño peppers, seeded and diced

4 cayenne peppers, seeded and diced

¼ cup fresh lemon juice

PORK WITH BLUE CHEESE POLENTA
& DROPPED PEACH HOT SAUCE

WE SPEND COUNTLESS HOURS preserving the seasons in a variety of different ways. Peach season is a special time of year, so we can't be overly picky—just because a peach isn't at its peak doesn't mean you can't find some way to make the most of it. For this recipe, we use overly ripe peaches (otherwise known as "dropped" or "B grade" peaches) to create a hot sauce that is sweet, sour, and spicy.—*K.S.*

YIELD: 6 TO 8 SERVINGS ⟶ **ACTIVE TIME: 40 MINUTES** ⟶ **TOTAL TIME: 6 HOURS**

1 Preheat the oven to 300°F. Season the pork generously with salt and pepper.

2 Place the pork shoulder in a large skillet and cook over medium-high heat, turning until it is browned all over.

3 Transfer the pork shoulder to a Dutch oven and add the onion, bay leaves, paprika, brown sugar, peppercorns, 4 cups of the stock, and mustard.

4 Cover the Dutch oven and place in the oven until the pork is fork tender, about 4 hours. Remove from the oven, let cool slightly, and then shred with a fork.

5 Approximately 1 hour before the pulled pork will be finished cooking, place the cornmeal, the remaining 3 cups of stock, and the water in a large pot. Bring to a boil over medium-high heat, reduce heat so that the mixture simmers, and cook, while stirring frequently, until the mixture is thick, about 40 minutes to 1 hour.

6 Add half of the butter and stir to combine. Stir half of the blue cheese into the pot, season with salt and pepper, and remove from heat. Set aside.

7 Once you have removed the pork shoulder from the oven, raise the oven temperature to 400°F.

8 Arrange the peaches skin side down on a baking sheet and place them in the oven. Cook until they begin to darken, about 10 minutes. You can also grill the peaches if you're after a slightly smokier sauce.

9 Remove the peaches from the oven and place in a medium saucepan. Add the vinegar, sugar, garlic, peppers, and lemon juice and bring to a simmer over medium-low heat. Simmer for 10 minutes, transfer the mixture to a blender, and puree until smooth.

10 Stir the remaining butter into the polenta and spoon the polenta into warmed bowls. Lay some of the pulled pork over it, and then top with the hot sauce and remaining blue cheese.

ROASTED CHICKEN THIGHS WITH TABBOULEH

BONELESS, SKINLESS CHICKEN MAKES PREP A LOT EASIER for many dishes, but you need both to stick around in this preparation. Searing the skin renders the fat and adds a tremendous amount of flavor, and cooking it on the bone ensures that the meat remains moist and tender.—*C.V.*

YIELD: 4 SERVINGS ⋯➤ **ACTIVE TIME: 25 MINUTES** ⋯➤ **TOTAL TIME: 1 HOUR**

FOR THE CHICKEN THIGHS

2 tablespoons olive oil

Salt and pepper, to taste

2 teaspoons paprika

2 teaspoons cumin

2 teaspoons ground fennel seeds

4 bone-in, skin-on chicken thighs

1 cup cherry tomatoes

2 garlic cloves, crushed

1 shallot, sliced

½ cup white wine

FOR THE TABBOULEH

1 cup bulgur wheat

2 cups water

1 shallot, halved

2 sprigs of thyme

1 tablespoon salt, plus more to taste

1 tablespoon chopped cilantro

1 tablespoon chopped parsley

2 tablespoons chopped scallions

1½ tablespoons fresh lime juice

½ cup diced tomato

½ cup diced cucumber

½ teaspoon minced garlic

3 tablespoons olive oil

Pepper, to taste

1 Preheat the oven to 450°F. Place the olive oil in a cast-iron skillet and warm over medium-high heat. Sprinkle salt, pepper, the paprika, cumin, and ground fennel on the chicken thighs. When the oil starts to smoke, place the thighs skin side down in the pan and sear until brown.

2 Turn the thighs over and place the pan in the oven. Cook until the internal temperature is 165°F, about 16 minutes. Halfway through the cooking time, add the tomatoes, garlic, and shallot to the pan.

3 When chicken is fully cooked, remove from the oven and transfer to a plate. Leave the vegetables in the pan, add the white wine, and place over high heat. Cook for 1 minute, while shaking the pan. Transfer the contents of the pan to the blender, puree until smooth, and season to taste. Set aside.

4 Prepare the tabbouleh. Place the bulgur, water, shallot, thyme, and salt in a saucepan and bring to a boil. Remove from heat, cover the pan with foil, and let sit until the bulgur has absorbed all the liquid. Fluff with a fork, remove the shallot and thyme, and add the remaining ingredients. Stir to combine and season with salt and pepper.

5 To serve, place some of the tabbouleh on each plate. Top with a chicken thigh and spoon some of the puree over it.

GRILLED CHICKEN PANINIS WITH
SUNDRIED TOMATO AIOLI & GARDEN SALAD

CONSTRUCTING A DELICIOUS SANDWICH STARTS WITH QUALITY BREAD. Once you've got that in place, the rest is easy. This spin on the BLT came about during one of my bread-baking sprees, and it makes for a wonderfully hearty lunch.—*C.V.*

YIELD: 4 SERVINGS → **ACTIVE TIME: 30 MINUTES** → **TOTAL TIME: 1 HOUR**

FOR THE AIOLI

1 cup chopped sundried tomatoes

1 cup mayonnaise

1 tablespoon whole grain mustard

2 tablespoons chopped parsley

2 tablespoons sliced scallions

1 teaspoon white balsamic vinegar

1 teaspoon chopped garlic

2 teaspoons salt

1 teaspoon black pepper

FOR THE SALAD

5 oz. mixed greens

1 cucumber, sliced

1 cup cherry tomatoes, halved

1 shallot, sliced

Salt and pepper, to taste

¼ cup White Balsamic Vinaigrette
(see page 73)

FOR THE SANDWICHES

8 slices of Rustic White Bread
(see page 61)

8 slices of cheddar cheese

4 (6 oz.) grilled chicken breasts

12 slices of cooked bacon

1 cup arugula

1 Preheat a panini press.

2 Prepare the aioli. Place all of the ingredients in a mixing bowl and stir until combined.

3 Prepare the salad. Place the greens, cucumber, cherry tomatoes, and shallot in a salad bowl and toss to combine. Season with salt and pepper, add the dressing, and toss to evenly coat.

4 Spread some of the aioli on each slice of bread. Place a slice of cheddar on each slice of bread. Slice the chicken breasts and divide evenly between four pieces of the bread. Top the slices of chicken with 3 slices of bacon and ¼ cup of the arugula. Assemble the sandwiches with the other slices of bread.

5 Place the sandwiches in the panini press and press until the cheese has melted and there is a nice crust on the bread. Remove and serve with the salad.

NOTE: If you don't have a panini press, don't worry. Simply place 1 tablespoon of olive oil in a sauté pan and warm over medium-high heat. Place a sandwich in the pan, place a cast-iron skillet on top so it is pressing down on the sandwich, and cook until golden brown. Turn the sandwich over and repeat.

CHILLED CORN SOUP
WITH SHRIMP SALAD & BASIL OIL

ON A HOT DAY AT THE HEIGHT OF CORN SEASON, this chilled soup is the perfect appetizer—especially when the corn cobs are utilized to make a flavorful stock.—*C.V.*

YIELD: 4 TO 6 SERVINGS ⇢ **ACTIVE TIME: 45 MINUTES** ⇢ **TOTAL TIME: 4 HOURS**

FOR THE SOUP

8 ears of corn, husked, silk removed, and rinsed

5 tablespoons unsalted butter

1 yellow onion, sliced

2 teaspoons chopped garlic

1½ tablespoons salt, plus 1 teaspoon

1 cup heavy cream

12 cups Corn Stock (see sidebar)

1 cup basil

⅓ cup canola oil

FOR THE SALAD

1 cup cooked shrimp, chilled and diced

½ cup reserved corn kernels

2 teaspoons lemon zest

2 teaspoons fresh lemon juice

½ cup diced cucumber

2 teaspoons sliced basil

1 teaspoon sliced chives

1 teaspoon mayonnaise

1 teaspoon salt

¼ teaspoon paprika

1 Preheat the oven to 400°F.

2 Place the ears of corn on a baking sheet, place it in the oven, and bake for 25 minutes. Remove from oven and let cool. When cool enough to handle, cut the kernels from the cobs and reserve the cobs for the stock (see sidebar). Reserve ½ cup of kernels for the salad and set the rest aside. Prepare the Corn Stock.

3 Place the butter in a large pot and melt it over medium heat. Add the onion, garlic, and teaspoon of salt and cook until the onion is translucent. Add the corn, cream, stock, and remaining salt and bring to a boil. Reduce heat and simmer until the corn is very tender, 15 to 20 minutes. Transfer the soup to a blender, puree until smooth, season to taste, and set aside until cool. When the soup has cooled completely, place it in the refrigerator.

4 Prepare the salad. Place all of the ingredients in a mixing bowl and toss to combine. Place in the refrigerator until ready to serve.

5 Place the basil and oil in a blender and puree on high, about 1 minute. Strain through cheesecloth or a coffee filter and discard the solids. The oil can be stored for 1 week.

6 When ready to serve, ladle the soup into bowls and top with spoonfuls of the salad. Drizzle with the infused oil and serve.

CORN STOCK

YIELD: 12 CUPS · ACTIVE TIME: 15 MINUTES
TOTAL TIME: 1 HOUR AND 30 MINUTES

8 corn cobs, kernels removed
1 bay leaf
1 sprig of thyme
½ teaspoon black pepper
14 cups water

1   Place all of the ingredients in a stockpot
    and bring to a boil over medium-high
    heat. Reduce heat and simmer for
    45 minutes.

2   Strain, discard the solids, and let cool
    before using in the soup.

RASPBERRY & TOMATO GAZPACHO
WITH MINT LEAVES

VERY FEW THINK OF SOUP DURING THE SUMMER, though that will change if you start whipping this up with some regularity. The smoky element added by the roasted tomatoes is a lovely counter to the sweetness of the raspberries. —*K.S.*

YIELD: 4 TO 6 SERVINGS ⋯ **ACTIVE TIME: 10 MINUTES** ⋯ **TOTAL TIME: 4 TO 24 HOURS**

2 to 3 large heirloom tomatoes

1 cup raspberries

2 garlic cloves

½ cup peeled and diced cucumber

2 teaspoons fresh lemon juice

2 tablespoons olive oil

1 red bell pepper, seeded and chopped

Salt and pepper, to taste

Mint leaves, for garnish

Heavy cream, for garnish (optional)

1 Preheat the oven to 425°F.

2 Place the tomatoes on a baking sheet and bake until they start to break down and darken, about 10 to 15 minutes. Remove from the oven and let cool slightly.

3 Place the tomatoes and the remaining ingredients in a blender and puree until smooth. Transfer the mixture to the refrigerator for at least 3 hours, though 24 hours in the refrigerator is recommended.

4 When ready to serve, ladle into bowls, season with salt and pepper, and garnish with mint leaves and, if desired, approximately 1 tablespoon of heavy cream.

MUSHROOM & SUMMER VEGETABLE PIZZA

PIZZA IS AWESOME. As a vehicle for so many delicious toppings, it is always a great way to use up those extra vegetable scraps and still keep even the pickiest of eaters happy.—*K.S.*

YIELD: 4 SERVINGS ••• **ACTIVE TIME: 30 MINUTES** ••• **TOTAL TIME: 1 HOUR AND 30 MINUTES**

FOR THE SAUCE

3 lbs. plum tomatoes

1 tablespoon oregano

2 teaspoons minced fresh thyme leaves

1 tablespoon olive oil

Salt and pepper, to taste

2 cups water

FOR THE DOUGH

1 cup warm water (104°F to 112°F)

1 tablespoon active dry yeast

1 teaspoon sugar

1 tablespoon olive oil

2½ cups "00" or all-purpose flour (Caputo "00" flour preferred), plus more for dusting

1 teaspoon salt

FOR THE PIZZA

4 oz. mushrooms, sliced (cremini or oyster preferred)

2 summer squash, sliced thin

1 bunch of spinach

4 oz. fresh mozzarella, sliced

½ cup shredded mozzarella

Leaves from 1 bunch of basil

1   Place all of the ingredients for the sauce in a saucepan and cook over medium-low heat until the tomatoes have broken down, about 45 minutes. Remove from heat and let cool for at least 15 minutes.

2   When cool, transfer to a blender and puree until the desired consistency has been achieved.

3   Return the sauce to the saucepan and simmer over low heat until it has thickened slightly. Remove from heat and set aside.

4   Preheat the oven to 450°F.

5   Prepare the dough. Place the water, yeast, and sugar in a large mixing bowl and stir gently. Let the mixture sit until it begins to bubble, about 7 to 10 minutes.

6   Add the olive oil to the mixture and stir. Add the flour and salt and stir until a dough forms. Remove the dough from the bowl and transfer to a flour-dusted work surface. Knead the dough until it is smooth, about 7 to 10 minutes.

7   Shape the dough into a ball and then roll out to desired size and shape.

8   Place the dough on a greased pan and prick it with a fork, which will prevent air pockets from forming. Place the dough on the lowest rack of your oven and bake for 5 to 7 minutes, until the dough starts to develop color. Remove and preheat the oven to 500°F.

9   Spread the sauce on the prepared crust, top with the vegetables, cheese, and basil, and place in the oven. Bake until the crust is golden brown and the cheese is bubbly, about 15 to 20 minutes. Remove from the oven and let cool slightly before slicing.

RASPBERRY PIE BARS

EVEN AMIDST THE SUMMER BOUNTY, working with berries is always inspiring, as their sweet smell encapsulates the season. These bars are simple, but when you use fresh fruit that is picked at its peak, you get a dessert that no one can resist.—*K.S.*

YIELD: 12 TO 24 BARS ⋯•⋯ **ACTIVE TIME: 30 MINUTES** ⋯•⋯ **TOTAL TIME: 1 HOUR**

---

2 balls of Leaf Lard Piecrust dough (see page 262)

7 cups fresh raspberries

2 cups sugar, plus more to taste

⅔ cup all-purpose flour

2 tablespoons fresh lemon juice

Pinch of salt

1 egg, beaten

1 Preheat the oven to 350°F and grease a 15 x 10-inch baking pan with a rim.

2 Roll out one of the balls of dough so that it fits the pan. Place it in the pan, press down to ensure that it is even, and prick the dough with a fork. Roll out the other ball of dough so that it is slightly larger than the pan.

3 Place the raspberries, sugar, flour, lemon juice, and salt in a mixing bowl and stir until well combined. Spread this mixture evenly across the dough in the baking pan.

4 Place the top dough over the filling and trim any excess. Brush the top with the egg and sprinkle with additional sugar. Place the bars in the oven and bake until golden brown, about 40 minutes. Remove from the oven and let cool before slicing.

ROASTED STRAWBERRY HANDPIES
WITH CINNAMON GLAZE

WHEN STRAWBERRY SEASON IS UPON US our minds reel with possible uses for them. They hold a particular magic for me, and I make sure to bask in the taste of that first berry. Roasting strawberries draws out the flavors that are hiding deep down, guaranteeing that these handpies will be a revelation for all who happen upon them. —*K.S.*

YIELD: 8 SERVINGS ⋯ **ACTIVE TIME: 40 MINUTES** ⋯ **TOTAL TIME: 2 HOURS**

---

3 quarts fresh strawberries, hulled and sliced

1 cup sugar

2 teaspoons fresh lemon juice

1 tablespoon cornstarch

½ tablespoon water

1 ball of Leaf Lard Piecrust dough (see page 262)

2 eggs, beaten

1½ cups powdered sugar, sifted

3 to 4 tablespoons whole milk

1 teaspoon cinnamon

1 Preheat the oven to 400°F.

2 Place the strawberries on a baking sheet and bake in the oven until they start to darken and release their juice, about 20 to 30 minutes. If you prefer, you can bake them for up to an hour. Cooking the strawberries for longer will caramelize the sugars and lend them an even richer flavor.

3 Remove the strawberries from the oven and place them in a saucepan with the sugar and lemon juice. Bring to a simmer over medium heat and cook for 20 minutes, until the mixture has thickened slightly.

4 Place the cornstarch and water in a small cup and stir until there are no lumps in the mixture. Add to the saucepan and stir until the mixture is syrupy. Remove from heat.

5 Roll out the dough to the desired thickness, cut it into two squares, and then cut each square into quarters. Spoon some of the strawberry mixture into the center of each quarter.

6 Take a bottom corner of each pie and fold to the opposite top corner. Press down to ensure that none of the mixture leaks out and then seal the edge with a fork. Place the pies on a baking sheet and brush them with the beaten eggs.

7 Place in the oven and bake until golden brown, about 20 to 30 minutes.

8 While the pies are cooking, place the powdered sugar, milk, and cinnamon in a bowl and stir until well combined.

9 Remove the pies from the oven, brush them with the sugar-and-cinnamon glaze, and allow to cool before serving.

BLUEBERRY & BANANA BREAD PUDDING

WITH ALL THE BREAD that I bake, I tend to have a lot of scraps that I toss in the freezer. This delicious bread pudding, which features some buttermilk to balance out the sweetness of the rum caramel, is one of the places those scraps find a home.—*C.V.*

YIELD: 4 TO 6 SERVINGS ⋯ **ACTIVE TIME: 1 HOUR** ⋯ **TOTAL TIME: 2 HOURS**

FOR THE BREAD PUDDING

1 banana

3 eggs

¾ cup brown sugar

½ cup heavy cream

½ cup milk

¼ cup buttermilk

1½ teaspoons vanilla extract

½ teaspoon salt

6 cups cubed Sourdough Bread
(see page 147)

1½ cups blueberries

FOR THE RUM CARAMEL

½ cup sugar

¼ cup dark rum, plus 2 tablespoons

¼ cup heavy cream, warmed

1 tablespoon unsalted butter

1 teaspoon salt

FOR THE WHIPPED CREAM

1 cup heavy cream

2 tablespoons confectioners' sugar

½ teaspoon salt

1   Place the banana, eggs, and brown sugar in a mixing bowl and mix with a handheld mixer on medium-high until the mixture is smooth and creamy.

2   Place the cream, milk, buttermilk, vanilla, and salt in a separate bowl and whisk to combine. Pour this mixture into the banana-and-egg mixture and beat until combined.

3   Place the pieces of bread in the bowl and toss until all the pieces are coated. Let the bread soak until the majority of the liquid has been absorbed, 30 to 45 minutes.

4   Preheat the oven to 375°F and grease a 9 x 5-inch loaf pan. Add the blueberries to the soaked bread and stir until evenly distributed. Pour the mixture into the loaf pan, cover with foil, and place it in the oven. Bake for 25 minutes, remove the foil, and bake for an additional 20 minutes.

5   While the bread pudding is in the oven, prepare the rum caramel. Place the sugar and ¼ cup of rum in a small saucepan and cook over medium heat until the mixture acquires an amber color. Reduce the heat and add the heavy cream, stirring constantly to incorporate it. Add the remaining rum, butter, and salt, remove from heat, and pour into a heatproof container.

6   Prepare the whipped cream. Place the cream, confectioners' sugar, and salt in a mixing bowl and beat until just before stiff peaks form.

7   Remove the bread pudding from the oven, drizzle with the rum caramel, and top with the whipped cream.

YOGURT WITH WHEY–FERMENTED BERRIES

THIS RECIPE CAME ABOUT ON A WARM DAY when I didn't have time to eat a proper breakfast and some leftover berries, kombucha, and yogurt were all I had in my fridge. I tossed them together and while enjoying the result I marveled at the complexity fermentation can add to even the simplest dishes. Whey is the watery mixture you see on top of yogurt, and it contains a lot of beneficial bacteria. Add it to some berries and let the mixture sit for a few days—you'll be so taken by the transformed flavor that health will be the furthest thing from your mind.—*K.S.*

YIELD: 10 TO 15 SERVINGS ⋯ **ACTIVE TIME: 5 MINUTES** ⋯ **TOTAL TIME: 5 TO 7 DAYS**

4 cups Homemade Yogurt
(see page 290), plus more for serving

2 pints of your preferred berries

1   Position a cheesecloth–lined sieve over a large bowl. Pour the yogurt into the sieve and press down to remove as much liquid as possible. You should have approximately 1 cup of liquid, which is the whey you will use to ferment the berries. Set the whey and the strained yogurt aside.

2   Place the berries in a large, sterilized jar. Cover with the whey and then cover the jar with a piece of cloth and secure with a rubber band. Let the jar sit at room temperature for 5 to 7 days. You will see bubbles form and rise to the top as the mixture ferments.

3   When ready to use, strain the mixture and serve the fermented berries over yogurt. Store any excess berries in the refrigerator for up to 1 week.

NOTE: The strained yogurt resulting from Step 1 will be very thick and rich. It can be whipped with olive oil to create a Mediterranean-style yogurt known as *labneh*.

HONEY–GINGER FROZEN YOGURT
WITH CARAMELIZED PLUMS

REALIZING THAT GINGER, HONEY, AND PLUMS are incredibly complementary to one another, I started looking for a preparation that featured all three. One night I had a hankering for a frosty treat and recognized that this frozen yogurt was the perfect vehicle for this powerful trio.—*C.V.*

YIELD: 4 SERVINGS ⋯⋯ **ACTIVE TIME: 15 MINUTES** ⋯⋯ **TOTAL TIME: 4 HOURS AND 30 MINUTES**

2½ cups Greek yogurt

½ cup evaporated milk

¼ teaspoon vanilla extract

1 teaspoon grated ginger

2 tablespoons light corn syrup

½ teaspoon salt

⅓ cup honey

½ cup sugar

2 plums, pitted and chopped into ½-inch pieces

4 tablespoons unsalted butter

1 Place the yogurt, evaporated milk, vanilla, ginger, corn syrup, salt, and honey in a mixing bowl and stir to combine. Pour the mixture into an ice cream maker and churn until the desired texture has been reached. Transfer to the freezer and freeze for at least 4 hours.

2 When ready to serve, place the sugar in a bowl and dip the pieces of plum into it until they are completely coated.

3 Place the butter in a large skillet and melt over medium heat. Add the pieces of plum and cook until golden brown all over, about 5 minutes.

4 Scoop the frozen yogurt into bowls and top with the caramelized plums.

BLUEBERRY & BASIL JAM

A COUPLE OF YEARS AGO, Chris and I had a ton of blueberries left over after a dinner, and anyone who knows us knows that we hate wasting food. As we ferried boxes of them down a dirt lane on the farm, we passed a huge patch of basil and inspiration struck: blueberry-and-basil jam. Be sure to lay a few jars of this away for the winter—it'll help on those days when the gray has nearly ground you down.—*K.S.*

YIELD: 20 TO 30 SERVINGS ••• **ACTIVE TIME: 10 MINUTES** ••• **TOTAL TIME: 1 HOUR AND 30 MINUTES**

3 quarts blueberries

Leaves from 1 bunch of basil, minced

2 teaspoons fresh lemon juice

2 cups sugar

½ cup water

1 Place all of the ingredients in a large pot and bring to a boil, while stirring frequently, over medium-high heat.

2 Once the mixture has come to a boil, reduce the heat and simmer, while stirring frequently, until the mixture has reduced by half and is starting to thicken, about 1 hour. Remove from heat and let it thicken and set as it cools. If the jam is still too thin after 1 hour, continue to simmer until it is the desired consistency.

3 Serve with an assortment of crackers and cheeses or slather on toast or pancakes. Store in the refrigerator for 1 week or see page 271 for instructions on canning.

ROSÉ SORBET

UNWINDING WITH A GLASS OF CHILLED ROSÉ is one of my favorite summer pastimes. That inclination got us thinking about another of our favorite amusements: making ice creams and sorbets. Combine the two, and you get this special treat. —*K.S.*

YIELD: 6 SERVINGS ⋯ **ACTIVE TIME: 10 MINUTES** ⋯ **TOTAL TIME: 28 TO 38 HOURS**

1⅓ cups sugar

1 (750 ml) bottle of Rosé

1 cup water

1 Place all of the ingredients in a saucepan and cook, while stirring, over medium-low heat until the sugar is completely dissolved. Raise the heat and bring to a boil.

2 Remove from heat and let cool completely. Cover and place the mixture in the refrigerator for 24 hours.

3 After 24 hours, pour the mixture into an ice cream maker and churn until the desired texture has been reached.

4 Transfer to the freezer and freeze for at least 4 hours before serving, though 8 to 10 hours in the freezer is recommended.

NOTE: An ice cream maker is a must for this and the other ice cream-adjacent preparations in this book. While not an essential kitchen appliance, a more-than-serviceable one from Cuisinart is available for around $40. Considering the price of a premium pint at the grocery store, that investment will be well worth it.

QUARK PANNA COTTA WITH ROSÉ RASPBERRY SAUCE

A LOT OF PEOPLE ARE UNFAMILIAR WITH QUARK, so I always grab some whenever I see it and think of ways that I can remedy this undeserved lack of attention. Panna cotta, which I fell in love with while working at an Italian restaurant, ended up being the perfect vehicle to spread the gospel of this delightful, tangy cheese.—*C.V.*

YIELD: 6 SERVINGS → **ACTIVE TIME: 40 MINUTES** → **TOTAL TIME: 24 HOURS**

FOR THE PANNA COTTA

2½ cups cream

⅔ cup whole milk

⅔ cup sugar

½ teaspoon salt

1 teaspoon vanilla extract

2 cups quark

½ oz. gelatin (2 envelopes)

6 tablespoons honey

Raspberries, for garnish

Toasted almonds, for garnish

Mint leaves, for garnish

FOR THE SAUCE

2 cups Rosé

⅓ cup sugar

¼ teaspoon salt

2 cups raspberries

1 Place the cream, milk, sugar, salt, and vanilla in a saucepan and bring to a boil over medium heat, taking care that the mixture does not boil over. Remove from heat.

2 Place the quark in a small mixing bowl and ladle about 1 cup of the mixture in the saucepan into the bowl. Whisk to combine and then pour the tempered quark into the saucepan.

3 Bring the mix back to a boil and then remove from heat. Place the gelatin in a large mixing bowl and pour the creamy mixture into it, while whisking constantly to prevent lumps from forming. Pour into the serving dishes and place in the refrigerator to set overnight.

4 Approximately 2 hours before you will serve the panna cotta, prepare the sauce. Place the Rosé in a small saucepan and cook over medium-high heat until it has reduced by half. Add the remaining ingredients, bring the mixture to a boil, and then reduce heat and simmer for 20 minutes. Transfer the mixture to a blender and puree until smooth. Strain through a fine sieve and place the sauce in the refrigerator to cool completely.

5 When the panna cottas are set, pour 1 tablespoon of honey over each serving. Pour the sauce on top of the honey and garnish with raspberries, toasted almonds, and mint.

FALL

⫶ FALL ⫶

WE'RE HARD-PRESSED to think of anything more iconic than fall in New England. From the leaf peepers who travel from miles away to the apple pickers who descend on our region like a swarm of locusts, fall is a time for celebration and harvest. The smell of warm apple cider wafting in the chilly air is a sure sign that the best time of the year is upon us.

In our early days at The Farmers Dinner we struggled with all of the different types of produce that were available in a given season. But we learned, often through firsthand experience. We processed turkeys at Loudonshire Farm. We worked with farms like Kimball Fruit Farm, which produces 41 styles of heirloom apples. We've learned that summer shouldn't hog the spotlight, as fall is really the time of abundance, as well as our busiest time of year.

All of this is coupled with the sense of urgency that autumn ushers in. We scramble to grab all that we can because we know that when the first hard frost hits, everything dies. As farms are filled with customers looking to carve pumpkins, we are selecting different styles of squashes like the Blue Hubbard, Delicata, Fairy Tale, and Long Island Cheese. We are cross-utilizing produce with the understanding that we are almost in winter's icy grasp. This urgency is echoed in our preparations as well. As we struggle to preserve everything we can, we battle the elements in a balancing act of time versus availability.

The beginning of fall is filled with warmth. As fall continues its descent into winter, the air changes dramatically. The start of the season is filled with the delicate sweetness of corn and tomatoes. By the end, you are left with hearty, earthy vegetables like brassicas (such as broccoli and kale) and squashes.

◄•►

SOURDOUGH BREAD

SOURDOUGH IS JUST FOUR INGREDIENTS—water, starter, salt, and flour—but it has a complexity that is unmatched. If you have not made real artisan bread before, I highly suggest that you start to learn, because it will change your life.—*K.S.*

YIELD: 1 LARGE LOAF ⟶ **ACTIVE TIME: 20 MINUTES** ⟶ **TOTAL TIME: 30 HOURS**

400 g filtered water (78°F)

600 g bread flour, plus more for dusting

200 g Sourdough Starter (see page 291)

8 g salt

1 Combine the water and the flour in a bowl and stir until no dry clumps remain and the dough has come together slightly. Cover with plastic wrap and let rest for 30 minutes.

2 Add the Sourdough Starter and salt to the dough. Knead for 10 minutes, until the dough is smooth and elastic. Place the dough in a bowl, cover with plastic wrap, and store in a naturally warm place for 4 hours.

3 Place the dough on a flour-dusted work surface and fold the left side of the dough to the right, fold the right side of the dough to the left, and fold the bottom toward the top. Form into a rough ball, return to the bowl, cover with plastic wrap, and let rest for 30 minutes.

4 After 30 minutes, place the ball of dough on a floured surface and repeat the folds made in Step 3. Form the dough into a ball, dust it with flour, and place it in a bowl with the seam facing up. Dust a clean kitchen towel with flour, cover the bowl with it, and place the bowl in the refrigerator overnight.

5 Approximately 2 hours before you are ready to bake the bread, remove it from the refrigerator and allow it to come to room temperature.

6 Preheat oven to 500°F. Place a covered Dutch oven in the oven as it warms.

7 When the dough is at room temperature and the oven is ready, remove the Dutch oven from the oven and carefully place the ball of dough into the Dutch oven. Score the top of the dough with a very sharp knife or razor blade, making a long cut across the middle. Cover the Dutch oven, place it in the oven, and bake for 25 minutes.

8 Remove the Dutch oven, lower the oven temperature to 480°F, remove the lid, and bake the bread for another 25 minutes. Remove from the oven and let cool for 2 hours before slicing.

BROWN BREAD

MY MOTHER FREQUENTLY MADE BROWN BREAD to serve with franks and beans when I was a child, and I hated it. Couldn't imagine anyone actually enjoying it. Eventually, I started making it from scratch, which led me to appreciate the rich flavor that allowed the recipe to make its way from the Colonial era to the modern world. Now, I'm in love with brown bread. I'm betting it's just a matter of time before you are as well.—*K.S.*

YIELD: 6 SERVINGS ⟶ **ACTIVE TIME: 15 MINUTES** ⟶ **TOTAL TIME: 1 HOUR TO 2 HOURS AND 30 MINUTES**

Butter, for greasing

½ cup rye flour

½ cup all-purpose flour

½ cup finely ground cornmeal or flint corn

½ teaspoon allspice

½ teaspoon baking powder

½ teaspoon baking soda

½ cup blackstrap molasses

¾ cup buttermilk

1 Preheat the oven to 325°F and grease a loaf pan or a coffee can with butter.

2 Sift the dry ingredients into a mixing bowl. Place the molasses and buttermilk in a separate mixing bowl and stir to combine. Add the wet mixture to the dry mixture and stir until well combined.

3 Pour the batter into the prepared container and cover with foil.

4 Place the loaf pan in the oven and bake for 40 to 45 minutes, until a knife inserted in the center comes out clean. If you are using a coffee can, place the can in a Dutch oven. Add boiling water so that three-quarters of the can is submerged, cover the Dutch oven, and place in the oven until a knife inserted in the center comes out clean, about 2 hours. If you are going to steam the bread in this manner—and with the light, moist bread that results, it's worth considering—make sure you check the water level after 1 hour, adding more if needed. Remove the bread from the oven and let cool completely before serving.

NOTE: If using a coffee can, you can also prepare the bread on the stovetop instead of the oven. Again, place the coffee can in the Dutch oven, cover three-quarters of the can with boiling water, cover the Dutch oven, and cook over medium heat for approximately 2 hours and 15 minutes.

PARKER HOUSE ROLLS

THESE LIGHT AND FLUFFY ROLLS, whose legend started in a Boston restaurant all the way back in the 19th century, are a staple around the holidays. If you want something a little different, try stuffing them with spicy sausage. You can thank us later.—*K.S.*

YIELD: 24 SERVINGS ⋯ **ACTIVE TIME: 1 HOUR** ⋯ **TOTAL TIME: 3 HOURS AND 30 MINUTES**

1 envelope of active dry yeast (about 2¼ teaspoons)

¼ cup warm water (109°F to 114°F)

1 cup whole milk

¼ cup vegetable shortening

3 tablespoons sugar

2 teaspoons kosher salt

1 large egg, at room temperature

3½ cups all-purpose flour, plus more for dusting

4 tablespoons unsalted butter, melted

Sea salt, to taste

1 In a small bowl, combine the yeast and warm water. Let the mixture stand for about 10 minutes, until it starts to foam.

2 Place the milk in a saucepan and warm over medium-low heat.

3 Place the shortening, sugar, and kosher salt in a mixing bowl and stir to combine. Add the warm milk and stir, making sure to break the shortening into small clumps. Whisk in the yeast-and-water mixture and the egg.

4 Add the flour and stir until a ball of dough forms. Place the ball of dough on a flour-dusted work surface and knead until the dough is smooth and elastic, about 10 minutes.

5 Transfer the dough to a lightly greased bowl, cover, and let rest in a naturally warm place until it has doubled in size, about 2 hours.

6 Grease a baking sheet and punch down the dough. Using a scale, measure out 1 to 2 oz. pieces of the dough (depending on the size you want) and use your hands to roll them into balls. Place the balls of dough on the baking sheet, making sure that the balls are pressing against each other. Brush the rolls with half of the melted butter, cover, and place in the refrigerator for 30 minutes.

7 Preheat the oven to 350°F. When it is ready, place the rolls in the oven and bake until golden, about 25 to 30 minutes. Remove from the oven, brush with the remaining butter, and sprinkle with sea salt before serving.

HERB-CRUSTED FOCACCIA

WE MAY HAVE AN ABUNDANCE OF HERBS at our fingertips, but it's never an issue finding ways to use them up. In the fall, one of our favorite recipients of this bounty of herbs is this slow-fermented focaccia, which is so good that you'll struggle to get it on the dinner table in one piece.—*K.S.*

YIELD: 12 SERVINGS → **ACTIVE TIME: 30 MINUTES** → **TOTAL TIME: 26 HOURS**

3¼ cups all-purpose flour

1½ cups water (78°F)

3 teaspoons salt

½ teaspoon active dry yeast

6 tablespoons olive oil

3 garlic cloves, sliced thin

Leaves from 2 sprigs of rosemary

Leaves from 2 sprigs of thyme

1 Place the flour, water, salt, and yeast in a large bowl and stir to combine. Mix well with your hands to ensure that all of the flour, salt, and yeast is incorporated.

2 Cover the bowl and let it sit in a naturally warm place for 24 hours, giving the dough time to come together and develop flavor. The dough should double in size after 24 hours.

3 After the dough has rested for 24 hours, preheat the oven to 450°F and grease a baking sheet.

4 Place the dough on the baking sheet and pat it into a ½-inch-thick rectangle. Brush the top with the olive oil and sprinkle the garlic, rosemary, and thyme all over.

5 Place in the oven and bake until golden brown, about 20 to 30 minutes. Remove and let cool slightly before serving.

KALE CHIPS

THESE CHIPS ARE HEALTHY, BUT NO LESS SATISFYING because of it. This seasoning blend is simply a suggestion based on my own personal preference; don't hesitate to experiment with your favorite spices.—*C.V.*

YIELD: 4 SERVINGS ⟶ **ACTIVE TIME: 10 MINUTES** ⟶ **TOTAL TIME: 30 MINUTES**

---

1 bunch of kale, stems removed

1 teaspoon salt

½ teaspoon pepper

½ teaspoon paprika

½ teaspoon dried parsley

½ teaspoon dried basil

¼ teaspoon dried thyme

¼ teaspoon dried sage

2 tablespoons olive oil

1 Preheat the oven to 350°F.

2 Tear the kale leaves into smaller pieces and place them in a mixing bowl. Add the remaining ingredients and work the mixture with your hands until the kale pieces are evenly coated.

3 Divide the seasoned kale between 2 parchment–lined baking sheets so that it sits on each in an even layer. Place in the oven and bake until crispy, 6 to 8 minutes. Remove and let cool before serving.

APPLE BUTTER

DESPITE THE NAME, THERE IS NO BUTTER in this preparation. Instead, the moniker refers to the texture, which is as smooth as butter. Be sure to include the skin and seeds of the apple, as they will enhance the flavor and help the mixture set. I like to use this spread for sandwiches and seasonal cheese boards, but you can confidently apply it anywhere you'd like. —*C.V.*

YIELD: 3 CUPS ·•· **ACTIVE TIME: 25 MINUTES** ·•· **TOTAL TIME: 2 HOURS**

3 cups brandy

5 lbs. apples

½ cup maple syrup

¼ cup brown sugar

1 teaspoon salt

½ teaspoon cinnamon

¼ teaspoon ground coriander

¼ teaspoon whole cloves

¼ teaspoon nutmeg

1   Place the brandy in a saucepan over medium-high heat and cook until it has reduced by half. Remove from heat and set aside.

2   Make sure to wash apples thoroughly. Cut them into quarters, place them in a stockpot, and cover with cold water. Bring to a boil over medium-high heat and then reduce the heat so that the apples simmer. Cook until tender, about 15 minutes, and then drain.

3   Preheat the oven to 225°F. Run the apples through a food mill and catch the pulp in a mixing bowl. Add the reduced brandy and the remaining ingredients, stir to combine, and transfer to a shallow baking dish.

4   Place the dish in the oven and bake, while stirring the mixture every 10 minutes, until all of the excess water has evaporated, about 1 to 1½ hours. Remove from the oven, transfer the mixture to a food processor, and puree until smooth.

CRANBERRY JAM

YIELD: 1½ CUPS · ACTIVE TIME: 5 MINUTES
TOTAL TIME: 1 HOUR

½ lb. fresh
cranberries

½ cup sugar

½ cup apple
cider

2 (¼-inch) slices
of ginger

1 teaspoon
orange zest

½ teaspoon salt

1   Place all of the ingredients in a small saucepan and bring
    to a boil. Reduce the heat so that the mixture simmers
    until the cranberries have broken down, 20 to 25 minutes.

2   Transfer the mixture to a mason jar and refrigerate until
    completely cool.

CHEESE BOARD WITH CRANBERRY JAM AND PICKLED HUSK CHERRIES

FREIGHTING A BOARD WITH A VARIETY of cheeses and a few other seasonal bites is one of the best, and easiest, ways to get a gathering off on the right foot. The beauty of it is that it can be plated beforehand, allowing the cheese to come to room temperature and exhibit every flavor lurking within.—*C.V.*

YIELD: 6 TO 8 SERVINGS ⇢ **ACTIVE TIME: 20 MINUTES** ⇢ **TOTAL TIME: 1 HOUR AND 30 MINUTES**

½ cup champagne vinegar

½ cup water

½ cup sugar

1 teaspoon salt

½ cup husk cherries, husks removed

12 oz. Cashel Blue (blue cheese)

12 oz. Cabot Clothbound Cheddar (hard-rind cheese)

12 oz. Von Trapp Farm Oma (soft-rind cheese)

12 slices of bread, toasted

¼ cup Cranberry Jam (see sidebar)

¼ cup Apple Butter (see page 156)

½ cup roasted peanuts

2 oz. honeycomb

1 Place the vinegar, water, sugar, and salt in a small saucepan and bring to a boil. Remove from heat, let cool slightly, and then pour over the husk cherries. Cover and transfer the mixture to the refrigerator for at least 1 hour.

2 While the husk cherries are pickling, arrange the cheeses, toasted bread, Cranberry Jam, Apple Butter, peanuts, and honeycomb on a serving board. Let stand at room temperature.

3 Add the pickled husk cherries and serve.

MUSHROOM TOAST WITH WHIPPED GOAT CHEESE

TOAST IS AS BASIC AS IT GETS, but you'd be surprised by how well it cleans up. This dish is a nod to our good friend William Dunkerley, an incredible forager and the owner of Dunk's Mushrooms in New Hampshire. He brought us some beautiful chestnut mushrooms when we started to partner with him, and their deep, nutty flavor has worked its way into a number of Farmers Dinners over the years.—*K.S.*

YIELD: 4 SERVINGS ⋯► **ACTIVE TIME: 10 MINUTES** ⋯► **TOTAL TIME: 45 MINUTES**

½ lb. chestnut mushrooms (or mushroom of your choice), sliced

2 tablespoons canola oil

Salt, to taste

4 thick slices of Sourdough Bread (see page 147)

½ cup heavy cream

½ cup goat cheese

2 oz. sunflower seeds

1 oz. fresh rosemary leaves

1 tablespoon honey

1 Preheat the oven to 400°F.

2 Place the mushrooms on a baking sheet, drizzle with half of the oil, and sprinkle with salt. Place the mushrooms in the oven and roast until they begin to darken, about 10 to 15 minutes.

3 Place the slices of bread on another baking sheet, brush the tops with the remaining oil, and sprinkle with salt. Place the slices of bread in the oven and bake until golden brown, about 10 minutes.

4 Place the cream in a mixing bowl and beat until stiff peaks begin to form. Add the goat cheese and beat until well combined.

5 Remove the mushrooms and bread from the oven and let cool for 5 minutes. Spread the cream-and-goat cheese mixture on the bread, top with the mushrooms, sunflower seeds, and rosemary, and drizzle with honey.

HONEY MUSTARD VINAIGRETTE

YIELD: 1 CUP · ACTIVE TIME: 5 MINUTES · TOTAL TIME: 5 MINUTES

¼ cup honey

2 tablespoons whole grain mustard

3 tablespoons apple cider vinegar

1 teaspoon salt

½ teaspoon black pepper

⅓ cup canola oil

Place all of the ingredients, except for the canola oil, in a small mixing bowl and whisk to combine. Add the oil in a slow stream and whisk until incorporated.

ROASTED BABY BEET, RADISH & APPLE SALAD
WITH BLUE CHEESE MOUSSE

BABY BEETS ARE PICKED IN THE SPRING to thin the field and leave room for other beets to grow, an early harvest that results in a flavor that is both rich and delicate. When you're working with something so uniquely delicious, it's important to keep it simple, and roasting these beets with a few aromatics is all they require. —*C.V.*

YIELD: 4 TO 6 SERVINGS ⇢ **ACTIVE TIME: 40 MINUTES** ⇢ **TOTAL TIME: 1 HOUR AND 45 MINUTES**

9 baby beets (3 each of red, golden, and pink)

3 tablespoons olive oil

3 teaspoons salt, plus more to taste

9 sprigs of thyme, leaves removed from 3

6 garlic cloves

6 tablespoons water

8 radishes with tops

6 oz. blue cheese

½ cup heavy cream

½ cup ricotta cheese

2 apples, peeled, cored, and diced

¼ cup Honey Mustard Vinaigrette (see sidebar)

Pepper, to taste

2 oz. honeycomb, for garnish

1 Preheat the oven to 400°F.

2 Form three sheets of aluminum foil into pouches. Group the beets according to color and place each group into a pouch. Drizzle each with the olive oil and sprinkle with salt. Divide the whole sprigs of thyme, garlic, and water between the pouches and seal them. Place the pouches on a baking sheet, place in the oven, and cook until fork tender, 45 minutes to 1 hour depending on the size of the beets. Remove the pouches from the oven and let cool. When cool enough to handle, peel the beets, cut into bite-sized pieces, and set aside.

3 Bring a pot of salted water to a boil and prepare an ice water bath in a mixing bowl. Remove the radish greens, wash them thoroughly, and set aside. Quarter the radishes.

4 Place the radishes in the boiling water, cook for 1 minute, and then transfer to the water bath until completely cool.

5 Place the blue cheese, heavy cream, ricotta, and thyme leaves in a food processor and puree until smooth. Set the mousse aside.

6 Place the beets, except for the red variety, in a salad bowl. Add the radishes, radish greens, and apples and toss to combine. Add half of the vinaigrette, season with salt and pepper, and toss to evenly coat.

7 Spread the mousse on the serving dishes. Place salad on top, sprinkle the red beets over the salad, drizzle with the remaining vinaigrette, and garnish with the honeycomb.

ROASTED BRUSSELS SPROUTS WITH BACON, BLUE CHEESE & PICKLED RED ONION

BRUSSELS SPROUTS HAVE A BAD REPUTATION with a lot of folks, but when seared and seasoned well, their savory, nutty flavor is a revelation, able to go toe-to-toe with rich ingredients like bacon and blue cheese.—*C.V.*

YIELD: 4 TO 6 SERVINGS ••• **ACTIVE TIME: 15 MINUTES** ••• **TOTAL TIME: 50 MINUTES**

1 cup champagne vinegar

1 cup water

½ cup sugar

2 teaspoons salt, plus more to taste

1 small red onion, sliced

½ lb. bacon, cut into 1-inch pieces

1½ lbs. Brussels sprouts, trimmed and halved

Pepper, to taste

4 oz. blue cheese, crumbled

1 Place the vinegar, water, sugar, and salt in a saucepan and bring to a boil. Place the onion in a bowl and pour the boiling liquid over the slices. Cover and allow to cool completely.

2 Place the bacon in a large sauté pan and cook, while stirring, over medium heat until crisp, about 7 minutes. Transfer to a paper towel–lined plate and leave the rendered fat in the pan.

3 Place the Brussels sprouts in the pan cut side down, season with salt and pepper, and cook over medium heat until they are a deep golden brown, about 7 minutes.

4 Transfer the Brussels sprouts to a platter, top with the pickled onions, bacon, and blue cheese and serve.

ROASTED BRUSSELS SPROUTS
WITH HOT HONEY & HAZELNUTS

WE'VE WORKED WITH A NUMBER OF APIARIES, and one day we came across one that was infusing their honey with the insanely hot Carolina Reaper pepper. When I tried it, I expected it to be nothing short of jarring. But the honey balanced the heat incredibly well. That pleasant surprise was the inspiration for this dish.—*K.S.*

YIELD: 4 SERVINGS ◦•◦ **ACTIVE TIME: 10 MINUTES** ◦•◦ **TOTAL TIME: 50 MINUTES**

1½ lbs. Brussels sprouts

3 tablespoons vegetable oil

Salt and pepper, to taste

½ cup Hot Honey (see page 274)

½ cup chopped hazelnuts

½ cup grated Parmesan cheese

1 Preheat oven to 400°F.

2 Trim the ends of the Brussels sprouts and then cut them in half. Place them in a bowl with the vegetable oil and salt and toss to combine.

3 Transfer the Brussels sprouts to a baking sheet, place them in the oven, and roast until they darken, about 30 to 40 minutes.

4 Remove the Brussels sprouts from the oven and let them cool slightly. Place them in a mixing bowl, add the honey, hazelnuts, and Parmesan and toss to combine. Season with salt and pepper and serve.

ROASTED CAULIFLOWER AU GRATIN

ONE SUREFIRE WAY TO GET PEOPLE EXCITED about cauliflower is poaching it in a flavorful stock and then caramelizing mild, nutty cheeses like Emmental and Parmesan on top.—*C.V.*

YIELD: 2 SERVINGS ➝ **ACTIVE TIME: 20 MINUTES** ➝ **TOTAL TIME: 1 HOUR AND 15 MINUTES**

2 cups wine

2½ cups water

⅓ cup salt

2 sticks of unsalted butter

6 garlic cloves, crushed

2 shallots, halved

1 cinnamon stick

3 whole cloves

1 teaspoon black peppercorns

1 sprig of sage

2 sprigs of thyme

1 head of cauliflower, leaves and stalk removed

1 cup shredded Emmental cheese

¼ cup grated Parmesan cheese

1 Place all of the ingredients, except for the cauliflower and cheeses, in a large saucepan and bring to a boil. Reduce heat so that the mixture simmers gently, add the head of cauliflower, and poach until tender, about 30 minutes.

2 While the cauliflower is poaching, preheat the oven to 450°F. Transfer the tender cauliflower to a baking sheet, place it in the oven, and bake until the top is a deep golden brown, about 10 minutes.

3 Remove from the oven and spread the cheeses evenly over the top. Return to the oven and bake until the cheeses have browned. Remove from the oven and let cool slightly before cutting it in half and serving.

15-oz. N.Y. strip steak

3 medium Idaho potatoes, peeled and cut into 1-inch pieces

1 tablespoon salt, plus more to taste

1 cup heavy cream

1 stick of unsalted butter

2 tablespoons canola oil

Cracked black pepper, to taste

3 sprigs of thyme

3 garlic cloves, crushed, plus 1 tablespoon minced garlic

1 shallot, halved

2 tablespoons olive oil

½ bunch of Swiss chard, stems removed and chopped

OVEN–ROASTED N.Y. STRIP STEAK
WITH WHIPPED POTATOES & SWISS CHARD

AS FALL TEMPERATURES GO from brisk to chilly, standing out by the grill doesn't seem quite as appealing. But that doesn't mean you have to say goodbye to the enchanting flavor of a quality steak.—*C.V.*

YIELD: 2 SERVINGS ⠂•► **ACTIVE TIME: 45 MINUTES** ⠂•► **TOTAL TIME: 1 HOUR AND 30 MINUTES**

1 Place the steak on a plate and let stand at room temperature for 20 to 30 minutes, as this will ensure that it cooks evenly. Preheat the oven to 475°F.

2 Place the potatoes in a saucepan, cover with cold water, and add the salt. Bring to a boil, reduce heat so that the potatoes simmer, and cook until tender, about 12 minutes. Strain and set aside.

3 Combine the cream and 6 tablespoons of the butter in a saucepan and heat until the butter is melted. Remove from heat, place the potatoes in the bowl of a stand mixer fitted with the whisk attachment, and add half of the cream-and-butter mixture. Whisk until the potatoes are smooth, adding more of the mixture as needed to achieve the desired consistency. Set aside.

4 Place a large cast-iron skillet over high heat and add the canola oil. Season the steak liberally with salt and cracked black pepper. When the oil begins to smoke, carefully place the steak in the skillet and cook for 2 minutes on each side.

5 When both sides of the steak have been seared, use kitchen tongs to turn the steak onto the side where the fat is. Hold the steak in place until the fat has rendered, about 2 minutes. Lay the steak flat in the pan and add the remaining butter, thyme, crushed garlic cloves, and shallot. Using a large spoon, baste the steak with the juices in the pan and cook for another minute. Remove from heat and place the steak on a wire rack resting in a baking sheet.

6 Place the steak in the oven and cook for 3 minutes. Remove and let stand for 8 to 10 minutes before slicing. The steak should be medium-rare, with an internal temperature of 145°F.

7 While the steak is resting, place the olive oil in a large sauté pan and warm over medium-high heat. When the oil starts to smoke, add the Swiss chard and minced garlic and cook until the chard is wilted. Season with salt and pepper.

8 To serve, cut the steak into desired portions and plate alongside the potatoes and Swiss chard.

YANKEE SHORT RIBS WITH ROASTED POTATOES & CARROTS

WE STUMBLED UPON THIS TWIST ONE DAY when a farm we were working with had too much short rib, an amazing cut from the brisket that benefits from cooking at low temperatures for a long time. Wanting to help them out, and prevent the wonderful fruits of their labor from going to waste, we decided to spice up a New England classic—the Yankee pot roast.—*K.S.*

YIELD: 4 SERVINGS ⟶ **ACTIVE TIME: 30 MINUTES** ⟶ **TOTAL TIME: 3 HOURS AND 30 MINUTES**

2 tablespoons canola oil

4 lbs. bone-in short ribs

Salt and pepper, to taste

2 large onions, sliced

4 carrots, diced

4 large potatoes, diced

8 cups Beef Stock (see page 193)

4 bay leaves

2 sprigs of rosemary

2 sprigs of thyme

½ cup red wine

1   Preheat the oven to 300°F.

2   Place the canola oil in a large skillet and warm it over medium-high heat. Pat the short ribs dry and season generously with salt.

3   Place the short ribs in the skillet and cook, while turning, until they are browned all over.

4   Transfer the browned short ribs to a Dutch oven with the onions, carrots, potatoes, stock, and bay leaves. Cover, place the Dutch oven in the oven, and cook until the short ribs are fork tender and the meat easily comes away from the bone, about 3 to 4 hours.

5   Remove from the oven, strain through a fine sieve, and reserve the cooking liquid. Set the short ribs and vegetables aside.

6   Place the reserved liquid in a pan with the rosemary, thyme, and red wine. Cook over high heat until the sauce has reduced and started to thicken.

7   Season with salt and pepper. Divide the short ribs and vegetables between the serving plates and spoon 2 to 3 tablespoons of the sauce over each portion.

CHICKEN BRINE

YIELD: 1½ GALLONS
ACTIVE TIME: 5 MINUTES
TOTAL TIME: 1 HOUR AND 30 MINUTES

¾ cup kosher salt

6 tablespoons sugar

6 cups water, at room temperature

½ tablespoon black peppercorns

5 garlic cloves, crushed

3 sprigs of thyme

1 bay leaf

12 cups ice-cold water

4 cups ice

1 Place all of the ingredients, except for the ice water and ice, in a large saucepan and bring to a boil, stirring to dissolve the sugar and salt. When these are dissolved, remove from heat.

2 Transfer to a 2-gallon container and add the ice water and ice. Let cool to room temperature before adding the chicken.

ROASTED WHOLE CHICKEN, ROOTS & BRASSICAS

ROASTING A WHOLE CHICKEN IS ONE OF THE CLASSIC SIMPLE MEALS. Brining the chicken beforehand elevates this satisfying standby to the realm of legend, producing moist flesh and a delectably crispy skin. Plus, you can use the leftovers for tacos and the carcass as the base of a delicious stock.—*C.V.*

YIELD: 2 TO 4 SERVINGS ⇢•⇠ **ACTIVE TIME: 30 MINUTES** ⇢•⇠ **TOTAL TIME: 24 HOURS**

1½ gallons Chicken Brine (see sidebar)

5-lb. chicken

Salt and pepper, to taste

1 teaspoon thyme leaves

1 cup diced sweet potato

1 cup diced Yukon Gold potato

1 cup diced celery root

1 cup diced carrots (½-inch pieces)

1 cup diced parsnips (½-inch pieces)

2 cups broccoli florets

2 cups cauliflower florets

2 tablespoons olive oil

1 Place the brine in a large stockpot, add the chicken, and place it in the refrigerator overnight. If needed, weigh the chicken down so it is submerged in the brine.

2 Remove the chicken from the brine and discard the brine. Place the chicken on a wire rack resting in a baking sheet and pat as dry as possible. Let sit at room temperature for 1 hour.

3 Preheat the oven to 450°F. Place the chicken in a baking dish, season lightly with salt and pepper, and sprinkle the thyme leaves on top. Place in the oven and roast until the juices run clear and the internal temperature in the thick part of a thigh is 160°F. Remove, transfer to a wire rack, and let cool for 15 to 20 minutes before carving. Leave the oven on.

4 Place the remaining ingredients in a mixing bowl, season with salt and pepper, and toss to evenly coat. Place on a parchment–lined baking sheet and roast until tender, about 15 minutes. Remove, carve the chicken, and serve alongside the roasted vegetable medley.

PORCHETTA

THIS DECADENT RECIPE WAS A NO–BRAINER for inclusion in this book. If you've never had this crispy, tender, rich wonder, prepare to be blown away.—*K.S.*

YIELD: 12 SERVINGS ⇢•⇠ **ACTIVE TIME: 30 MINUTES** ⇢•⇠ **TOTAL TIME: 2 DAYS**

5- to 6-lb., skin-on pork belly

1 tablespoon minced fresh rosemary leaves

1 tablespoon minced fresh thyme leaves

1 tablespoon minced fresh sage leaves

2 teaspoons garlic powder

Salt, to taste

1-lb. pork tenderloin (center cut preferred)

1 Place the pork belly skin side down. Using a knife, score the flesh in a diamond pattern. Rub the minced herbs and garlic powder into the flesh. Flip the pork belly over and poke small holes in the skin. Turn the pork belly over and rub salt into the flesh. Place the pork tenderloin in the center of the pork belly and then roll the pork belly up so that it retains its length. Tie the rolled pork belly securely with kitchen twine every ½ inch.

2 Transfer the pork belly to a rack with a pan underneath, place it in the fridge, and leave uncovered for 2 days. This allows the skin to dry out a bit. Pat the pork belly with paper towels occasionally to remove excess moisture.

3 Remove the pork belly from the refrigerator and let stand at room temperature for 1 to 2 hours.

4 Preheat the oven to 480°F. When the pork belly is at room temperature, place the rack and the pan in the oven and cook for 35 minutes, turning to ensure even cooking.

5 Reduce the oven temperature to 300°F and cook until a meat thermometer inserted into the center reaches 145°F, about 1 to 2 hours. The skin of the pork belly should be crispy. If it is not as crispy as you'd like, raise the oven's temperature to 500°F and cook until crispy. Remove from the oven and let stand for 15 minutes before slicing.

PORK & APPLE CASSEROLE

MY MOTHER MADE A VERSION of this for special occasions. But, stuck with the thin pork chops that were common at that time, the result was always over-cooked pork and apples that were too mushy. It was special mainly because of the love she had for those she was preparing it for. This is my take on her classic dish, which should wow anyone who happens past.—*K.S.*

YIELD: 4 SERVINGS ⟶ **ACTIVE TIME: 30 MINUTES** ⟶ **TOTAL TIME: 1 HOUR**

8 apples, sliced

2 teaspoons cinnamon

1 teaspoon nutmeg

¼ cup sugar

¼ cup all-purpose flour

Salt and pepper, to taste

¼ cup apple cider

1½-lb. pork tenderloin

2 tablespoons freshly ground rosemary leaves

2 tablespoons freshly ground thyme leaves

1 Preheat the oven to 325°F.

2 Place the apples, cinnamon, nutmeg, sugar, flour, and a pinch of salt in a mixing bowl and stir to combine. Transfer the mixture to a baking dish or Dutch oven and then add the apple cider.

3 Rub the pork tenderloin with the ground herbs and a pinch of salt and pepper. Place the pork on top of the apple mixture, cover, and place in the oven. Cook until a meat thermometer inserted into the center of the tenderloin registers 145°F, about 40 minutes.

4 Remove the pork tenderloin from the oven and slice. Serve on beds of the apple mixture.

JERK ACORN SQUASH WITH
BABY KALE SALAD & MAPLE VINAIGRETTE

AT KIMBALL FRUIT FARM in Pepperell, Massachusetts, there is a group of Jamaicans who are responsible for growing some of the best produce around. On the weekends, they sell the jerk chicken their homeland is famous for at the farm stand. Inspired by the flavors of the dish, and the rich culture responsible for it, I used those scintillating spices to spruce up a roasted squash.—*C.V.*

YIELD: 4 SERVINGS ⟶ **ACTIVE TIME: 25 MINUTES** ⟶ **TOTAL TIME: 2 HOURS**

FOR THE SQUASH & SALAD

2 Acorn squash

1 cup Jerk Marinade (see sidebar)

1 tablespoon olive oil

½ teaspoon salt

¼ teaspoon pepper

¼ teaspoon paprika

6 cups baby kale

½ cup dried cranberries

1 cup crumbled feta cheese

FOR THE MAPLE VINAIGRETTE

½ cup apple cider vinegar

½ cup maple syrup

1 teaspoon orange zest

2 teaspoons Dijon mustard

3 teaspoons salt

1 teaspoon black pepper

2 ice cubes
(see page 70 for note on ice cubes)

1½ cups vegetable oil

1 Preheat the oven to 400°F.

2 Cut the squash lengthwise, remove the seeds, and reserve them. Trim the ends of the squash so that each half can sit evenly, flesh side up, on a baking sheet. Score the flesh in a diamond pattern, cutting approximately ⅛ inch into the flesh. Brush some of the marinade on the squash and then fill the cavity with ⅓ cup. Place the baking sheet in the oven and bake until the squash is tender, about 45 minutes to 1 hour. As the squash is cooking, brush the flesh with the marinade in the cavity every 15 minutes. Remove from the oven and let cool. Lower the oven temperature to 350°F.

3 Run the seeds under water and remove any pulp. Pat the seeds dry, place them in a mixing bowl, and add the olive oil, salt, pepper, and paprika. Toss to combine and then place the seeds on a baking sheet. Place in the oven and bake until they are light brown and crispy, about 7 minutes.

4 Place the toasted seeds, kale, and cranberries in a salad bowl and toss to combine.

5 Prepare the vinaigrette. Place all of the ingredients, except for the vegetable oil, in a blender. Turn on high and add the oil in a slow stream. Puree until the mixture has emulsified. Season to taste and add to the salad bowl. Toss to coat evenly and top the salad with the crumbled feta.

6 To serve, place a bed of salad on each plate and place one of the roasted halves of squash on top.

JERK MARINADE

YIELD: 1 CUP
ACTIVE TIME: 10 MINUTES
TOTAL TIME: 10 MINUTES

¼ cup maple syrup

¼ cup brown sugar

1 tablespoon molasses

½ teaspoon cayenne pepper

1 teaspoon chili powder

1 teaspoon paprika

1 teaspoon cumin

½ teaspoon ground cloves

1 teaspoon cinnamon

½ teaspoon nutmeg

2 teaspoons salt

1 teaspoon pepper

2 teaspoons minced ginger

1 tablespoon chopped
thyme leaves

2 tablespoons sliced scallions

2 tablespoons diced shallot

1 tablespoon minced garlic

1 tablespoon fresh lime juice

Place all of the ingredients
in a blender and puree until
smooth.

SQUASH RISOTTO WITH BABY KALE, TOASTED WALNUTS & DRIED CRANBERRIES

RISOTTO IS SO MUCH MORE than a bowl of rice, particularly when you add the sweetness of Butternut squash, which brings the nutty flavor of Arborio rice to the fore.—*C.V.*

YIELD: 6 TO 8 SERVINGS ⇢ **ACTIVE TIME: 35 MINUTES** ⇢ **TOTAL TIME: 1 HOUR AND 20 MINUTES**

1 stick of unsalted butter

3 cups diced onions

1 small Butternut squash, peeled and diced

1 tablespoon salt, plus 2 teaspoons

3 cups milk

5 cups Roasted Vegetable Stock (see page 201)

2 cups Arborio rice

2 cups white wine

3 cups baby kale, stemmed and chopped

¾ cup toasted walnuts

½ cup dried cranberries

1 Place 2 tablespoons of the butter in a saucepan and melt over medium heat. Add half of the onions and cook until translucent. Add the squash, the tablespoon of salt, and the milk, reduce the heat to low, and cook until the squash is tender, about 20 minutes. Strain, discard the cooking liquid, and transfer the squash and onions to a blender. Puree until smooth and then set aside.

2 Place the vegetable stock in a saucepan, bring to a boil, and remove from heat.

3 Place the remaining butter in a large sauté pan with high sides and melt over medium heat. Add the remaining onions and cook until they are translucent. Add the rice and remaining salt and cook, while stirring constantly, until you can smell a toasted nutty aroma. Be careful not to brown the rice.

4 Deglaze the pan with the white wine and continue to stir until all the liquid has evaporated. Add the warmed stock in 1-cup increments and stir constantly until all of the stock has been incorporated. Add the squash puree and kale, stir to incorporate, and season to taste. Add the walnuts and dried cranberries and serve.

SWEET POTATO GNOCCHI WITH SAGE BROWN BUTTER

GNOCCHI, WHEN DONE PROPERLY, are light, soft, and full of flavor. To make sure this version captures the feeling of fall and still carries the pillowy texture that makes these dumplings so wonderful, I've used sweet potatoes and ricotta.—*C.V.*

YIELD: 6 SERVINGS ⟶ **ACTIVE TIME: 1 HOUR** ⟶ **TOTAL TIME: 2 HOURS AND 30 MINUTES**

2½ lbs. sweet potatoes

½ cup ricotta cheese

1 egg

2 egg yolks

1 tablespoon salt, plus more to taste

1 teaspoon pepper

3 tablespoons light brown sugar

2 tablespoons maple syrup

2 cups all-purpose flour, plus more as needed

1 cup semolina flour

2 tablespoons olive oil

1 stick of unsalted butter

1 tablespoon chopped sage leaves

2 cups arugula

½ cup toasted walnuts, chopped

1 Preheat the oven to 350°F. Wash the sweet potatoes, place them on a parchment–lined baking sheet, and use a knife to pierce several holes in the tops of the potatoes. Place in the oven and cook until they are soft all the way through, 45 minutes to 1 hour. Remove from oven, slice them open, and let cool completely.

2 Scrape the cooled sweet potato flesh into a mixing bowl and mash until smooth. Add the ricotta, egg, egg yolks, salt, pepper, brown sugar, and maple syrup and stir until thoroughly combined. Add the flours 1 cup at a time and work the mixture with your hands until incorporated. When touched, the dough should hold its shape and not stick to your hand. If it is too moist, add more all-purpose flour until the proper consistency has been achieved. Place the olive oil in a mixing bowl and set aside.

3 Transfer the dough to a lightly floured work surface and cut into 10 even pieces. Roll each piece into a long rope and cut the ropes into ¾-inch pieces. Use a fork to roll the gnocchi into desired shape and place the shaped dumplings on a lightly floured baking sheet.

4 Bring a large pot of salted water to a boil. Working in small batches, add the gnocchi to the boiling water and stir to keep them from sticking to the bottom. The gnocchi will eventually float to the surface. Cook for 1 more minute, remove, and transfer to the bowl containing the olive oil. Toss to coat and place on a parchment–lined baking sheet to cool.

5 Place the butter in a sauté pan and cook over medium heat until it begins to brown. Add the sage and cook until the bubbles start to dissipate. Place the arugula in a bowl and set aside.

6 Working in batches, add the gnocchi to the sauté pan, toss to evenly coat, and cook until they have a nice sear on one side. Transfer to the bowl of arugula and toss to combine. Plate and top with the toasted walnuts.

4 lbs. pork belly

3 bay leaves

3 cups apple cider

2 cinnamon sticks

2 teaspoons whole cloves

1 large onion, sliced

6 cups Chicken Stock (see page 236)

3 star anise pods

1 tablespoon peppercorns

2 carrots, chopped

2 celery stalks, chopped

1 lb. navy beans

8 cups water

Salt and pepper, to taste

1 cup Tomato Sauce (see page 198)

2 tablespoons brown sugar

2 tablespoons apple cider vinegar

Scraps of Brown Bread (see page 148)

2 tablespoons canola oil

NAVY BEAN SOUP WITH TWICE-COOKED PORK BELLY & BROWN BREAD CROUTONS

BRAISING THE PORK BELLY AND PRESSING IT OVERNIGHT locks in a ton of flavor, guaranteeing a mouthwatering dinner. The brown bread croutons are a small, but crucial, component, adding just a little crunch and just a little sweetness. —*K.S.*

YIELD: 6 SERVINGS ⟶ ACTIVE TIME: 40 MINUTES ⟶ TOTAL TIME: 30 HOURS

1 Preheat the oven to 300°F. Place the pork belly, bay leaves, apple cider, cinnamon sticks, cloves, onion, 2 cups of the stock, the star anise, peppercorns, carrots, and celery in a Dutch oven.

2 Cover the Dutch oven, place it in the oven, and cook until the pork belly shreds at the touch of a fork, about 3 to 4 hours.

3 Remove from the oven and place the pork belly, skin side up, in a shallow baking dish. Add enough of the cooking liquid to submerge half of the pork belly. Strain the remaining liquid and reserve it for another preparation. Discard the spices and vegetables.

4 Place a piece of parchment paper over the pork belly and place the dish in the refrigerator. Place a pan on top of the pork belly and add some weight to the pan so that it is pressing down on the pork belly. Store in the refrigerator for 24 hours.

5 Soak the navy beans overnight. Drain and reserve the liquid for another preparation.

6 Place half of the water in a large saucepan, add salt, and bring to a boil. Add the beans, cook until tender, and drain.

7 Place the cooked beans in a large saucepan with the remaining water, remaining stock, and Tomato Sauce and bring to a boil over medium-high heat. Reduce heat and let the mixture simmer for 30 minutes.

8 Add the brown sugar and apple cider vinegar, stir to incorporate, and simmer for 20 minutes.

9 While the soup is simmering, preheat the oven to 400°F. Remove the pork belly from the refrigerator and slice.

10 Cut the scraps of Brown Bread into cubes and place them in a mixing bowl with the canola oil. Toss to combine, season with salt, and place the pieces of bread on a baking sheet. Place the sheet in the oven and bake for 10 to 15 minutes, until crisp. Remove and let cool slightly.

11 Place a skillet over medium heat. Add the pork belly, skin side down, to the skillet and cook until golden brown. Turn the pork belly over and cook until the other side is also golden brown. Be careful while searing the pork belly, as it will splatter quite a bit.

12 Season the soup with salt and pepper and ladle it into warmed bowls. Top with the pork belly and the croutons before serving.

P.E.I. MUSSELS WITH PICKLED RAMPS

THE MUSSELS FROM PRINCE EDWARD ISLAND are some of the best in the world. They are naturally sweet and salty, and they'll readily suck up the flavor of the liquid you poach them in. Don't overlook the charred bread here, as it's a must for soaking up all of the leftover juices.—*C.V.*

YIELD: 4 SERVINGS ⋯ **ACTIVE TIME: 20 MINUTES** ⋯ **TOTAL TIME: 45 MINUTES**

1 lb. P.E.I. mussels

⅓ cup all-purpose flour

4 tablespoons unsalted butter

1 small shallot, chopped

2 garlic cloves, chopped

8 thin slices of fennel

½ cup cherry tomatoes

¼ cup white wine

¼ cup sliced Pickled Ramps (see sidebar)

Salt and pepper, to taste

4 slices of Rustic White Bread (see page 61)

1 tablespoon olive oil

2 tablespoons chopped parsley leaves, for garnish

1 Place the mussels in a large bowl, cover with water, add the flour, and let soak for 30 minutes to ensure that the mussels aren't sandy. Drain the mussels and debeard them.

2 Place half of the butter in a large sauté pan and melt over high heat. Add the shallot, garlic, fennel, and tomatoes and cook, while continually shaking the pan, until the aromatics begin to brown and the tomatoes begin to blister. Add the mussels and deglaze the pan with the wine. Allow the alcohol to cook off, about 30 seconds, and add then add the remaining butter. Toss to coat the mussels and emulsify the sauce. Add the Pickled Ramps and a small pinch of salt and pepper. When the majority of the mussels have opened, remove from heat and set aside. Discard any mussels that did not open.

3 Turn on the broiler. Drizzle the bread with the olive oil and sprinkle with salt and pepper. Place beneath the broiler until it starts to char. Remove from the oven and set aside.

4 Ladle the mussels and sauce into warmed bowls, garnish with parsley, and serve with the charred bread.

NOTE: To debeard the mussels, take a firm grip on the hair that is protruding from the shell and pull until it comes free.

PICKLED RAMPS

YIELD: 2 SERVINGS · ACTIVE TIME: 5 MINUTES
TOTAL TIME: 2 HOURS

½ cup champagne vinegar

½ cup water

¼ cup sugar

1½ teaspoons salt

¼ teaspoon fennel seeds

¼ teaspoon coriander seeds

⅛ teaspoon red pepper flakes

10 small ramp bulbs

1   Place all of the ingredients, except for the ramps, in a small saucepan and bring to a boil over medium heat.

2   Add the ramps, reduce the heat, and simmer for 1 minute. Transfer to a mason jar, cover with plastic wrap, and let cool completely. Once cool, cover with a lid and store in the refrigerator for up to 1 week.

CLAM CHOWDER WITH POTATO CHIPS

WHEN YOU THINK OF FOOD in New England, clam chowder is near the top of the list. As you'll see, it's worth the hype. This preparation hews to the classic version, featuring just a few tweaks.—*K.S.*

YIELD: 6 SERVINGS ⋯•► **ACTIVE TIME: 20 MINUTES** ⋯•► **TOTAL TIME: 50 MINUTES**

2 cups vegetable oil, plus 1 tablespoon

4 potatoes, 1 sliced thin, 3 diced

Salt and pepper, to taste

¾ cup pancetta, diced

1 large onion, diced

3 cups clam juice

1 cup milk

2 cups heavy cream

6 tablespoons unsalted butter

2 celery stalks, chopped

10 oz. clam meat, minced

Leaves from 2 sprigs of thyme, minced

1 teaspoon hot sauce

1 Place the 2 cups of vegetable oil in a Dutch oven and heat to 350°F.

2 Place the thinly sliced potato in the oil and fry until golden brown. Remove, place on a paper towel–lined plate, and sprinkle with salt.

3 Place the remaining vegetable oil and the pancetta in a large saucepan and cook over medium-low heat until brown.

4 Add the onion and cook until brown. Add the clam juice and the diced potatoes, raise the heat to medium, and cook until the potatoes are fork tender, about 10 minutes.

5 Add the milk, cream, butter, celery, clam meat, and thyme and simmer for 10 minutes.

6 Stir in the hot sauce and serve with the potato chips.

FRENCH ONION SOUP

THERE IS NOTHING LIKE SOUP IN THE FALL. This recipe is great if you've got a surplus of onions and some day-old bread you'd like to use up. With the addition of Sherry and maple syrup, no one will have any idea you're trying to be economical.—*K.S.*

YIELD: 6 SERVINGS ⤑ **ACTIVE TIME: 1 HOUR** ⤑ **TOTAL TIME: 2 HOURS AND 30 MINUTES**

3 tablespoons unsalted butter

7 large sweet onions, sliced

2 teaspoons salt

⅓ cup orange juice

3 oz. Sherry

Leaves from 3 sprigs of thyme, minced

7 cups Beef Stock (see sidebar)

3 garlic cloves, minced

2 teaspoons black pepper

6 slices of day-old bread

1 cup Gruyère cheese, shredded

1 cup Emmental cheese, shredded

1   Place the butter, onions, and salt in a Dutch oven and cook over low heat while stirring often. Cook until the onions are dark brown and caramelized, about 40 to 60 minutes.

2   Add the orange juice and Sherry to deglaze the pot. Use a wooden spoon to scrape any browned bits from the bottom.

3   Add the thyme, stock, garlic, and pepper, raise the heat to medium, and bring to a simmer. Simmer for 1 hour.

4   While the soup is simmering, preheat the oven to 450°F.

5   After 1 hour, ladle the soup into oven-safe bowls and place a slice of bread on top of each one. Divide the cheeses between the bowls, place them in the oven, and bake until the cheese begins to brown, about 10 to 15 minutes. Carefully remove the bowls from the oven and let cool for 10 minutes before serving.

BEEF STOCK

YIELD: 6 QUARTS
ACTIVE TIME: 30 MINUTES
TOTAL TIME: 5 HOURS

10 lbs. beef bones, or combination of beef, veal, and lamb bones

½ cup canola oil

1 leek, trimmed, washed, and cut into 1-inch pieces

1 celery stalk with leaves, cut into 1-inch pieces

10 quarts water

8 oz. tomato paste

8 sprigs of parsley

5 sprigs of thyme

2 bay leaves

1 teaspoon peppercorns

1 teaspoon salt

1 Preheat oven to 350°F.

2 Place bones on baking tray and cook until golden brown, about 45 minutes.

3 As bones cook, pour canola oil into a large stockpot and warm over low heat. Add vegetables and cook until any additional moisture has evaporated.

4 Add water, bones, tomato paste, aromatics, and salt to stockpot, raise heat to high, and bring to a boil.

5 Reduce heat and simmer for a minimum of 2 hours; ideally stock will cook for 4 hours.

6 When stock is finished cooking, strain through cheesecloth and place in refrigerator to cool.

7 Once cool, skim fat layer from top and discard. Use stock immediately or store in refrigerator or freezer.

PUMPKIN BISQUE WITH SPICED CRÈME FRAÎCHE

THE LONG ISLAND CHEESE PUMPKIN IS THE ONE OF THE OLDEST pumpkin varieties in the United States, but its meaty, dense flesh and sweet, earthy flavor make it ideal for this modern-leaning bisque.—*E.V.*

YIELD: 6 TO 8 SERVINGS ⟶ **ACTIVE TIME: 25 MINUTES** ⟶ **TOTAL TIME: 2 HOURS AND 15 MINUTES**

FOR THE BISQUE

1 Long Island Cheese pumpkin

6 tablespoons unsalted butter

2 yellow onions, sliced

1½ tablespoons chopped garlic

4 cups milk

1 cup heavy cream

2 tablespoons brown sugar

2 tablespoons salt, plus ½ teaspoon

1 tablespoon olive oil

¼ teaspoon black pepper

¼ teaspoon paprika

Maple syrup, for garnish

FOR THE CRÈME FRAÎCHE

1 cup crème fraîche

½ teaspoon cinnamon

⅛ teaspoon nutmeg

⅛ teaspoon ground cloves

1 tablespoon maple syrup

1 Preheat the oven to 350°F. Split the pumpkin in half lengthwise, remove the seeds, and reserve them. Place the halves of pumpkin cut side down on an aluminum foil–lined baking sheet.

2 Place the pumpkin in the oven and cook until the flesh is tender, about 40 minutes. Remove from the oven, taking care not to spill any of the juices, and let cool. Leave the oven on.

3 Place the butter in a saucepan and melt over medium-high heat. Add the onions and garlic and cook until the onions are translucent.

4 Add the milk, cream, sugar, and 2 tablespoons of salt and reduce the heat to medium. Scoop the flesh from the pumpkin and add it to the pan. Bring the soup to a boil and then reduce the heat so that it simmers. Cook, while stirring occasionally, for 20 minutes.

5 While the soup is simmering, run the reserved pumpkin seeds under water to remove any pulp. Pat them dry, place them on a baking sheet, drizzle with the olive oil, and sprinkle them with the remaining salt, pepper, and paprika. Place in the oven and bake until light brown and crispy, 6 to 8 minutes. Remove from the oven and set aside.

6 Prepare the crème fraîche. Place all of the ingredients in a bowl, stir to combine, and set aside.

7 Working in batches, add the soup to the blender and puree until smooth. Season to taste, ladle into bowls, and top each with a dollop of the crème fraiche, the toasted seeds, and a drizzle of maple syrup.

CURRY KURI SQUASH BISQUE

KURI IS A THIN-SKINNED, orange squash with a flavor similar to chestnuts. It sounds exotic, but you can find it at farmers markets all over New England. The curry powder is more than just a homonym here, adding the hint of sweet spice that we all crave in the fall.—*K.S.*

YIELD: 6 SERVINGS ⟶ **ACTIVE TIME: 30 MINUTES** ⟶ **TOTAL TIME: 2 HOURS**

1 large Kuri squash, quartered

1 large onion, sliced

2 tablespoons vegetable oil

Salt and pepper, to taste

2 tablespoons curry powder

4 tablespoons unsalted butter

1 cup cream

1 cup whole milk

2 sprigs of rosemary

2 sprigs of thyme

1 Preheat the oven to 400°F.

2 Place the squash and onion in a baking dish, drizzle with the oil, and season with salt. Place the dish in the oven and cook until the onion has browned, 15 to 25 minutes. Remove the dish from the oven, transfer the onion to a bowl, return the squash to the oven, and cook until tender, about 20 to 35 minutes. Remove the squash from the oven and let cool.

3 When the squash is cool enough to handle, scoop out the seeds. Scoop out the flesh and place it in the bowl with the onion.

4 Place the squash, onion, and remaining ingredients in a large saucepan and bring to a boil over medium-high heat. Reduce heat to low and let the mixture simmer, while stirring occasionally, for 15 to 20 minutes.

5 Remove the thyme and rosemary sprigs. Transfer the bisque to a blender and puree until desired consistency is achieved. Season with salt and pepper and ladle into warmed bowls.

NOTE: The toasted squash seeds make a lovely garnish for this soup. To do this, wash the seeds to remove any pulp and then pat them dry. Transfer them to a baking sheet, drizzle with olive oil, sprinkle with salt, and place the sheet in the oven. Cook until crispy and golden brown, 6 to 8 minutes.

TOMATO SAUCE

YIELD: 8 CUPS · ACTIVE TIME: 20 MINUTES
TOTAL TIME: 2 HOURS

4 lbs. tomatoes, quartered

1 large onion, sliced

15 garlic cloves, crushed

2 teaspoons thyme leaves

2 teaspoons oregano leaves

2 tablespoons olive oil

1½ tablespoons salt

1 teaspoon black pepper

2 tablespoons chopped basil

1 tablespoon chopped parsley

1   Place all of the ingredients, except for the basil and parsley, in a large saucepan and cook, while stirring constantly, over medium heat. When the tomatoes give up their liquid and begin to break down, reduce heat to low and cook for about 1½ hours, until the flavor has developed to your liking.

2   Stir in the basil and parsley and season to taste. The sauce will be chunky. If a smoother texture is preferred, transfer to a blender and puree.

MINESTRONE

THIS HEARTY SOUP IS A TIMELESS CLASSIC. Understated in nature and complex in flavor, it is a great way to use up any vegetable scraps that you have lying around. —*C.V.*

YIELD: 6 SERVINGS ⟶ **ACTIVE TIME: 30 MINUTES** ⟶ **TOTAL TIME: 24 HOURS**

---

1 cup cattle beans, soaked overnight

2 sprigs of thyme

Salt and pepper, to taste

3 tablespoons olive oil

1 cup diced celery

1 cup diced carrots

1½ cups diced onions

2 tablespoons sliced garlic

2 cups sliced cabbage

1½ cups Tomato Sauce (see sidebar)

8 cups Roasted Vegetable Stock (see page 201)

1 Parmesan rind (optional)

Parmesan cheese, grated, for garnish (optional)

1 Drain the beans and place them in a saucepan with the sprigs of thyme. Cover with cold water, bring to a boil, and then reduce the heat. Simmer the beans until they are tender, about 1½ hours. Drain the cooked beans and reserve the cooking liquid. Season the beans with salt and pepper and let cool.

2 Place the olive oil in a large saucepan and warm over medium heat. When the oil starts to smoke, add the celery, carrots, onions, and garlic and cook, while stirring constantly, until the onions are translucent. Add the cabbage and cook until tender.

3 Add the sauce, stock, 4 cups of the reserved cooking liquid, and, if using, the Parmesan rind. Bring to a boil and then reduce the heat. Simmer for 30 minutes and then taste to see if a rich flavor has developed. If not, continue to simmer until it does.

4 Season with salt and pepper, ladle into warmed bowls, and garnish with grated Parmesan, if desired.

HEIRLOOM TOMATO AND SMOKED CHEDDAR SOUP

THE END OF TOMATO SEASON is always bittersweet, as it also signals the end of summer. This creamy soup is one of the easiest ways to handle the transition to the crisp, cool air of fall.—*CV.*

YIELD: 6 SERVINGS → **ACTIVE TIME: 20 MINUTES** → **TOTAL TIME: 1 HOUR AND 15 MINUTES**

2 sticks of unsalted butter

1 small red onion, sliced

3 celery stalks, sliced

10 garlic cloves, sliced

1 tablespoon salt, plus more to taste

½ cup all-purpose flour

8 heirloom tomatoes, chopped

3 cups Tomato Sauce (see page 198)

1 tablespoon tomato paste

4 cups Roasted Vegetable Stock (see sidebar)

1 Parmesan rind (optional)

1 cup heavy cream

4 oz. smoked cheddar cheese, grated

10 basil leaves, sliced thin

Pepper, to taste

1 Place the butter in a large saucepan and melt over medium heat. Add the onion, celery, garlic, and salt and cook until the onion is translucent.

2 Add the flour and cook, while stirring constantly to ensure that it does not brown too quickly, until it gives off a nutty aroma. Add the tomatoes, Tomato Sauce, tomato paste, stock, and, if using, the Parmesan rind. Stir to incorporate and let the soup come to a boil. Reduce heat and let simmer for 30 minutes. Taste to see if the flavor is to your liking. If not, continue to simmer until it is.

3 Stir the cream, cheddar, and basil into the soup. Remove the Parmesan rind, transfer the soup to a blender, and puree until smooth. Season with salt and pepper and ladle into warmed bowls.

ROASTED VEGETABLE STOCK

YIELD: 8 CUPS · ACTIVE TIME: 25 MINUTES
TOTAL TIME: 9 TO 11 HOURS

4 cups chopped onion
3 cups chopped carrots
3 cups chopped celery
3 sprigs of thyme
1 teaspoon whole black peppercorns
1 bay leaf

1   Preheat the oven to 400°F.

2   Place half of the vegetables on baking sheets, place them in the oven, and cook until browned, about 20 minutes.

3   Put the roasted vegetables and remaining ingredients in a large pot and cover with water. Bring the stock to a boil and then reduce heat. Simmer for 8 to 10 hours, strain, and discard the solids. Let cool before using.

GRAPE-NUT CUSTARD PUDDING

IN MY HOMETOWN THERE WAS A LEGENDARY RESTAURANT where I frequently ate as a child. And while that restaurant eventually closed down, the food retains its mythic status in the town. One of the most beloved dishes was this dessert, a recipe I was incredibly fortunate to get my hands on. After testing it out many times, I made some slight alterations and landed on this preparation, which the whipped cream is essential to.—*K.S.*

YIELD: 12 SERVINGS ⟶ **ACTIVE TIME: 10 MINUTES** ⟶ **TOTAL TIME: 1 HOUR**

4 cups whole milk, warmed

½ cup Grape-Nuts

5 eggs

1 teaspoon vanilla extract

½ cup sugar

1 teaspoon cinnamon

1 whole nutmeg

Whipped cream, for garnish

Maple syrup, for garnish

1 Preheat the oven to 350°F.

2 Place the milk, Grape-Nuts, eggs, vanilla, and sugar in a bowl and stir until well combined.

3 Transfer the mixture to a baking dish and then place the dish in a pan of hot water. Place in the oven and cook for 15 minutes.

4 Remove the baking dish from the oven and stir the pudding. Return to the oven and cook until golden brown and a knife inserted into the center comes out clean, about 15 minutes.

5 Remove from the oven, sprinkle with cinnamon, and grate the nutmeg over the top. Allow to cool completely.

6 When mixture is cool, top each serving with a dollop of whipped cream and a drizzle of maple syrup.

INDIAN PUDDING

THIS RECIPE DATES BACK TO THE 18TH CENTURY, when New Englanders who had a hankering for the hasty pudding they left behind in Britain had to make the most of what was available, meaning molasses and cornmeal (which the colonists referred to as "Indian flour"). When we get a hankering for Indian Pudding, we like to go see Chuck Cox at Tuckaway Farm in New Hampshire, and purchase some flint corn. The high quality and exceptionally deep flavor of Chuck's product makes the dish.—*K.S.*

YIELD: 8 SERVINGS ⋯ **ACTIVE TIME: 10 MINUTES** ⋯ **TOTAL TIME: 9 TO 27 HOURS**

3 cups whole milk

1 cup heavy cream

½ cup flint corn (or cornmeal)

½ cup blackstrap molasses

½ cup light brown sugar

½ teaspoon ground ginger

½ teaspoon nutmeg

½ teaspoon allspice

2 teaspoons cinnamon

2 teaspoons salt

5 eggs

5 tablespoons unsalted butter

Whipped cream, for serving

1 Preheat the oven to 275°F and grease a baking dish.

2 Place the milk in a large saucepan and cook over medium-high heat until it comes to a boil. Remove the saucepan from heat and set aside.

3 Place all of the remaining ingredients, except for the eggs, butter, and whipped cream, in a mixing bowl and stir to combine. Whisk this mixture into the heated milk.

4 Place the saucepan over medium-low heat and cook, while stirring, until the mixture begins to thicken. Remove the saucepan from heat.

5 Crack the eggs into a bowl and beat with a whisk. Add ½ cup of the hot molasses-and-cornmeal mixture and whisk to combine. Continue whisking in ½-cup increments of the mixture until all of it has been incorporated. Add the butter and whisk until it has been incorporated.

6 Pour the mixture into the prepared baking dish. Place the dish in a pan of water, place in the oven, and bake until it is set, about 2 hours.

7 Remove from the oven and let cool. When cool, transfer to the fridge for 6 to 24 hours. Serve with the whipped cream.

ROASTED PARSNIP ICE CREAM

AT FIRST GLANCE, YOU MAY BE TAKEN ABACK by the prospect of root vegetables in ice cream. But we wouldn't include it in this book if it wasn't delicious. In fact, it's my absolute favorite ice cream. And, by using the pieces you would typically discard, you can feel good while you indulge.—*K.S.*

YIELD: 6 SERVINGS ⟶ **ACTIVE TIME: 20 MINUTES** ⟶ **TOTAL TIME: 14 TO 32 HOURS**

1½ cups heavy cream

1½ cups whole milk

3 to 4 cups roasted parsnip trimmings (the stuff you typically throw away)

Pinch of salt

⅔ cup sugar

5 egg yolks

1 Place the cream, milk, roasted parsnip pieces, and salt in a saucepan and cook over medium heat until the mixture starts to bubble. Remove it from heat and allow the mixture to steep for 30 minutes to 1 hour.

2 Strain the mixture through a fine sieve, while pressing down on the pieces of parsnip to remove as much liquid as possible. Place the liquid in a saucepan and bring to a simmer. Discard the pieces of parsnip.

3 Place the sugar and eggs in a bowl and whisk until combined.

4 Once the liquid is simmering, add a little bit of the milk-and-cream mixture to the egg-and-sugar mixture and whisk constantly. Add the milk-and-cream mixture in small increments until all of it has been incorporated, while taking care not to cook the eggs.

5 Return the mixture to the saucepan and cook over low heat, while stirring, until it is thick enough to coat the back of a wooden spoon. Remove from heat and let cool. When cool, cover and transfer to the refrigerator for 6 to 24 hours.

6 When you are ready to make ice cream, add the mixture to your ice cream maker and churn until the desired consistency has been achieved. Place the churned cream in the freezer for a minimum of 6 hours before serving.

CRANBERRY SORBET

AUTUMN MAKES MOST PEOPLE THINK OF SWEET AND SPICY, but for me, the tart taste of cranberries exemplifies the essence of the season.—*C.V.*

YIELD: 3 CUPS ⇢ **ACTIVE TIME: 20 MINUTES** ⇢ **TOTAL TIME: 5 HOURS**

½ lb. fresh cranberries

2¾ cups water

13 tablespoons sugar

1 cup orange juice

½ teaspoon cornstarch

1 Place the cranberries, 9 oz. of the water, and 5 tablespoons of the sugar in a medium saucepan and cook over medium heat until all of the cranberries pop open. Transfer the mixture to the blender and puree until smooth, starting at a low speed and increasing to high. Strain through a fine sieve and place in the refrigerator until chilled.

2 Place the remaining water and sugar in a saucepan and bring to a boil, while stirring, until the sugar is dissolved. Remove from heat and let cool completely. This is your simple syrup.

3 Place the cranberry puree, simple syrup, orange juice, and cornstarch in a bowl and mix until combined.

4 Pour the mixture into an ice cream maker and churn until the desired texture has been reached.

5 Transfer to the freezer and freeze for at least 4 hours, until it is set.

CRANBERRY & APPLE CRISP

KEITH AND I ARE ALIGNED ON OUR LOVE OF APPLE CRISP in the fall. The key is finding an apple that doesn't turn to mush as it bakes, and I've found that the balanced sweetness and firm texture of the Honeycrisp apple works best.—*C.V.*

YIELD: 4 SERVINGS ⟶ **ACTIVE TIME: 20 MINUTES** ⟶ **TOTAL TIME: 1 HOUR**

¾ cup granulated sugar

¼ cup all-purpose flour, plus 2½ tablespoons

1 teaspoon salt

⅓ teaspoon cinnamon

½ teaspoon nutmeg

⅛ teaspoon ground cloves

2½ cups diced Honeycrisp apples

1 cup fresh cranberries

¾ cup oats

¼ cup brown sugar

2 teaspoons orange zest

6 tablespoons unsalted butter, melted

1   Preheat the oven to 375°F. Place the sugar, 2½ tablespoons of flour, half the salt, cinnamon, nutmeg, and cloves in a mixing bowl and stir to combine. Add the apples and cranberries and toss until evenly coated.

2   Place the oats, the remaining flour, brown sugar, remaining salt, orange zest, and half of the melted butter in a mixing bowl and stir to combine. Add the remaining butter and stir until incorporated.

3   Divide the apple-and-cranberry mixture between four ramekins, leaving ½ inch at the top of each. Top with the crumble, place the ramekins on a baking sheet, and bake until the top is golden brown and the filling is bubbly, 35 to 40 minutes. Remove and let cool slightly before serving.

SMOKED APPLE CRISP

FOR ME, APPLE CRISP IS FALL. I have a number of fond memories of roasting apples over a bed of coals and watching the fruit transform itself into a sweet, smoky treat. This preparation brings that idealized reminiscence to life.—*K.S.*

YIELD: 8 TO 10 SERVINGS ⤍ **ACTIVE TIME: 20 MINUTES** ⤍ **TOTAL TIME: 2 HOURS**

1 cup hickory or applewood chips

4 lbs. apples, sliced (Baldwin or Granny Smith recommended)

1 cup sugar

1 cup all-purpose flour

3 teaspoons cinnamon

1 cup oats

1 cup brown sugar

¼ teaspoon baking soda

¼ teaspoon baking powder

1 stick of unsalted butter, softened

1 teaspoon nutmeg

1 Soak the wood chips in a bowl of water 1 hour before you are ready to cook the apples.

2 Bring your smoker to 250°F. Place the soaked wood chips in the smoking tray and place the apples in the smoker. Smoke for 8 to 10 minutes. If you are using a grill to smoke the apples, prepare one side of the grill for indirect heat. To do this, bank the coals to one side of a charcoal grill or leave one of the burners of a gas grill off. When the grill is 300°F, place the soaked wood chips on the coals or in a smoker box for a gas grill and place the apples over indirect heat. Cover the grill and cook for 8 to 10 minutes. Remove the apples and set aside.

3 Preheat the oven to 350°F. Place the sugar, flour, 2 teaspoons of the cinnamon, oats, brown sugar, baking soda, and baking powder in a mixing bowl and mix by hand until combined. Add the butter and mix until the butter has been incorporated and the mixture is a coarse, crumbly meal.

4 Place the apples in a bowl with the remaining cinnamon, the nutmeg, and half of the crumble. Toss to combine. Transfer this mixture into a greased baking dish, top with the remaining crumble, and bake until golden brown, about 35 to 45 minutes.

APPLE CIDER

ONE OF THE FIRST SIGNS that summer is over in New England is the air becoming filled by the warm smell of spices steeping in apple cider. Bring a little bit of that warmth into your own home with this easy and delicious preparation.—*E.V.*

YIELD: 8 CUPS ••• **ACTIVE TIME: 10 MINUTES** ••• **TOTAL TIME: 2 HOURS AND 15 MINUTES**

12 apples, quartered

1 tablespoon sliced ginger

1 cinnamon stick

¼ cup maple syrup

2 tablespoons brown sugar

1 orange, halved

1 Place all of the ingredients in a large stockpot and cover with cold water.

2 Bring to a boil over medium-high heat. Cover the stockpot and reduce the heat so that the mixture simmers. Cook for 2 hours.

3 After 2 hours, remove the pot from heat, strain, and either discard the solids or reserve them for another preparation. Enjoy hot or let cool and serve over ice. The cider will keep in the refrigerator for 1 week.

PEAR GALETTE WITH MAPLE CARAMEL

THIS RUSTIC, FREE-FORM TART is a perfect introduction to pie making, featuring a flaky crust, spices that capture the scent of autumn and bring out the best in the Anjou pear, and a rich caramel that ties everything together.—*C.V.*

YIELD: 6 TO 8 SERVINGS •••• **ACTIVE TIME: 45 MINUTES** •••• **TOTAL TIME: 1 HOUR AND 45 MINUTES**

FOR THE DOUGH

1½ cups all-purpose flour, plus more for dusting

1 teaspoon cinnamon

¼ teaspoon nutmeg

¼ teaspoon ground cloves

1½ teaspoons salt

2 teaspoons brown sugar

2 sticks of unsalted butter

½ cup ice-cold water

1 egg yolk, beaten

FOR THE FILLING

¼ cup granulated sugar

2 teaspoons cinnamon

3 Anjou pears, cored and cut into ¼-inch slices

1½ tablespoons lemon zest

½ tablespoon minced ginger

2 tablespoons butter, cut into small pieces

FOR THE MAPLE CARAMEL

1 stick of unsalted butter

1 cup dark brown sugar

½ teaspoon kosher salt

½ cup maple syrup

1. Place the flour, cinnamon, nutmeg, cloves, salt, and sugar in a bowl and whisk to combine. Divide the butter into tablespoons and place them in the freezer for 15 minutes.

2. Place the flour mixture and the frozen pieces of butter in a food processor and pulse four to five times to incorporate. Gradually add the water and pulse until the dough has just come together. Remove from the food processor, place on a lightly floured work surface, and knead until all of the ingredients are thoroughly incorporated. Place in the refrigerator for at least 20 minutes before rolling out.

3. Preheat the oven to 400°F and prepare the filling. Place the sugar and cinnamon in a bowl, stir to combine, and set aside. Place the pears, lemon zest, minced ginger, and butter in a bowl and gently toss, being careful not to break the slices of pear.

4. Place the dough on a lightly floured work surface and roll out into a 12-inch circle that is approximately ¼ inch thick. Place the pear slices on the dough in layers, making sure to leave 1½ inches of dough at the edges. Sprinkle each layer with the sugar-and-cinnamon mixture before adding the next one.

5. Fold the edge of the dough over the filling and crimp. Brush this crust with the egg yolk and sprinkle with the sugar-and-cinnamon mixture. Carefully lift the galette onto a parchment-lined baking sheet, place it in the oven, and bake until the crust is golden brown and the pears are tender, about 25 minutes.

6. While the galette is baking, prepare the maple caramel. Place the butter in a saucepan and melt over medium heat. Add the sugar and salt and cook, while stirring constantly, until the sugar is dissolved, about 5 minutes. Add the maple syrup and cook until the mixture is smooth and thick.

7. Remove the galette from the oven, drizzle the maple caramel over the top, and let cool for 5 to 10 minutes before serving.

WINTER

⋛ WINTER ⋛

FOR US, WINTER is a time to reflect and appreciate the bounty of the preceding seasons. Hot summer days wouldn't be as treasured if not for the contrast of cold, seemingly endless winter nights. It is a time to bake, can, and find new and creative ways to utilize the items you preserved.

The holiday season can be chaotic around New England. Yankee swaps are replaced with New Year's celebrations in a matter of days. But for the farmer, it is a time to slow down and begin preparations for next year. Gone are the bounties of fall. Now is the time of Christmas trees and root cellar produce, with farms like Lull Farm in Hollis, New Hampshire, switching from pumpkins to pine wreaths. The drastic change in temperature and availability causes us to respect and cherish the moments we had, and will have in the upcoming year.

In the winter, we continue to host events in the form of "pop up" dinners in restaurants across New England. When we plan menus we look first to the root cellar. Ingredients like sunchokes, rutabagas, celeriac, and parsnips adorn our menus. We crave hearty dishes and find innovative ways to put fresh spins on different items. Many people believe that winter means that nothing grows in New England. One of the questions we often get is, "What do you cook in winter?" Dairy, meat, root cellar vegetables, and hydroponics are just a few local sources of food in the winter months.

There is beauty in the stillness of a snowfall while bread bakes in the oven. We are blessed with so much diversity in terms of weather and food that slowing down and having an opportunity to appreciate a snowfall, or a parsnip, is something we often take for granted. Winter forces us to reflect on the passage of the year. It forces us to not waste food. It forces us indoors, where we cozy up beside a warm fire. Yes, come February we love to complain about the subzero temperatures, but soon the cycle repeats itself and the warmth of the dawning spring will be upon us.

Food should be about sharing. Winter teaches us to share the bounty of the seasons with our neighbors. Far too often we fail to see the wonder available in the simple act of opening a jar of jam preserved at the height of strawberry season. The pop of the lid ushers in memories of warm summer air, as well as the labor and love that went into the process. Winter presents challenges. But it also presents opportunities to experiment, learn, and grow.

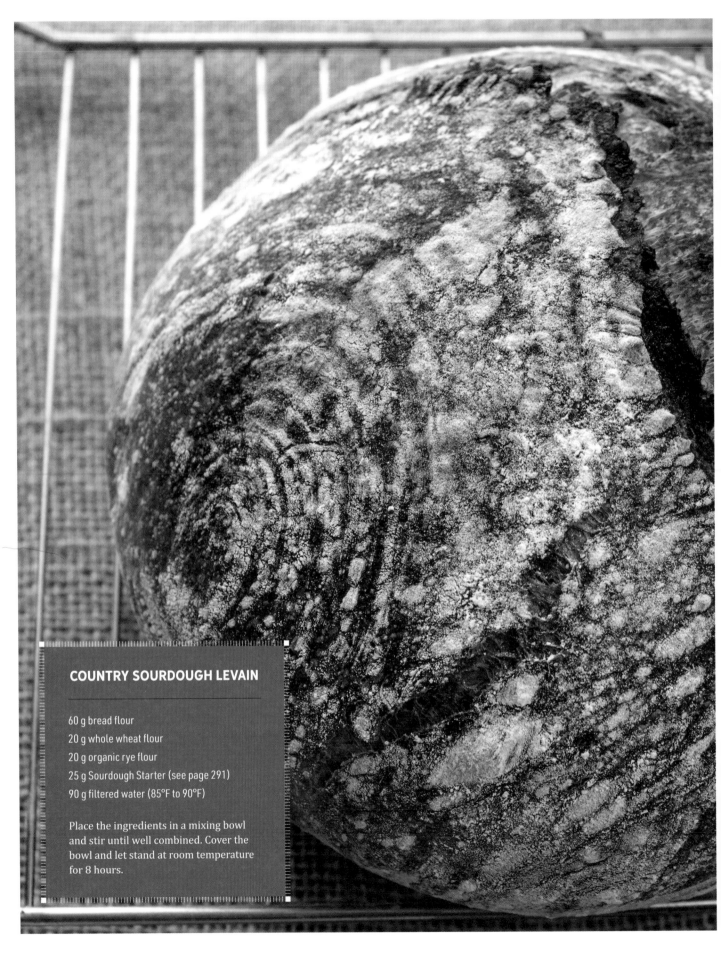

COUNTRY SOURDOUGH LEVAIN

60 g bread flour

20 g whole wheat flour

20 g organic rye flour

25 g Sourdough Starter (see page 291)

90 g filtered water (85°F to 90°F)

Place the ingredients in a mixing bowl and stir until well combined. Cover the bowl and let stand at room temperature for 8 hours.

COUNTRY SOURDOUGH BREAD

THIS SOURDOUGH USES A FEW DIFFERENT FLOURS to give the bread a rustic, wheaty taste. Keep in mind that the hydration level in your levain needs to increase when you bake with whole wheat flour, to balance out the additional density.—*K.S.*

YIELD: 1 LARGE LOAF ⋅•⋅ **ACTIVE TIME: 20 MINUTES** ⋅•⋅ **TOTAL TIME: 2 DAYS**

651g filtered water (78°F)

500 g bread flour, plus more for dusting

100 g whole wheat flour

50 g organic rye flour

10 g salt

220 g Country Sourdough Levain (see sidebar)

1   Place 650 grams of the water and the flours in a bowl and mix until all of the flour has been incorporated. Cover with plastic wrap and let stand for 1 hour.

2   Add the salt, the levain, and the remaining water to the dough. Transfer the dough to a flour-dusted work surface and knead until the dough is smooth and elastic, about 10 minutes.

3   Place the kneaded dough in a bowl and cover with plastic wrap. Place the bowl in a naturally warm spot and let stand for 4 hours.

4   Transfer the dough to a flour-dusted work surface. Fold the left side of the dough to the right, fold the right side of the dough to the left, and fold the bottom toward the top. Form into a rough ball, return to the bowl, cover with plastic wrap, and let rest for 30 minutes.

5   After 30 minutes, place the ball of dough on a floured surface and repeat the folds made in Step 4. Form the dough into a ball, dust it with flour, and place it in a bowl with the seam facing up. Dust a clean kitchen towel with flour, cover the bowl with it, and place the bowl in the refrigerator overnight.

6   Remove the dough from the refrigerator 2 hours before baking and allow it to come to room temperature.

7   Preheat the oven to 500°F. Place a covered Dutch oven in the oven as it warms.

8   When the oven is ready, remove the Dutch oven and carefully place the dough into it. Score the top with a very sharp knife or razor blade, making one long cut across the middle. Cover the Dutch oven and place the bread in the oven.

9   Cook for 25 minutes, remove the Dutch oven, and lower the oven's temperature to 480°F. Remove the Dutch oven's cover, return the bread to the oven, and bake for another 25 minutes. If it is done, the bread should sound hollow when tapped.

10 Remove the bread from the oven, transfer to a wire rack, and allow to cool for 2 hours before slicing.

CORNMEAL CRÊPES

BY TAKING A TRADITIONAL JOHNNYCAKE AND NODDING toward French cuisine, this preparation acknowledges the wonderful contributions that people of French ancestry have made to life in New England. You can fill these crêpes with almost anything, but they're particularly wonderful with fruit and real maple syrup.—*K.S.*

YIELD: 6 SERVINGS ⇢ **ACTIVE TIME: 40 MINUTES** ⇢ **TOTAL TIME: 1 HOUR AND 20 MINUTES**

¾ cup finely ground cornmeal

1¼ cups all-purpose flour

1 teaspoon salt

1 teaspoon cinnamon

1¾ cups whole milk

¼ cup cream

3 eggs

4 tablespoons melted unsalted butter, plus more as needed

1 Sift the cornmeal, flour, salt, and cinnamon into a bowl.

2 Place the milk, cream, eggs, and 3 tablespoons of the butter in another bowl and beat until combined. Add the wet mixture to the dry mixture, stir to combine, and let stand for 30 to 40 minutes.

3 Place the remaining butter in a skillet and warm over medium heat. Stir the batter and pour about ⅓ cup into the skillet. Tilt and swirl the pan so that a thin layer of the batter covers the entirety of it.

4 Cook until the edges of the crêpe start to lift away from the pan and turn slightly golden. Turn the crêpe over and cook for another 20 to 30 seconds. Transfer cooked crêpes to a plate and cover. If the skillet becomes too dry, add butter as needed.

ROASTED CHESTNUTS

WHEN I WAS A KID, my parents would occasionally boil and eat chestnuts at home, much to my confusion as I didn't like the taste. Later I learned that they are a delicacy in their home country of Haiti. Now I have a better appreciation for them and find it hard to resist their buttery, sweet flavor. Don't worry, you don't need an open fire to roast them, as the song suggests. I like to steam them in foil packets so I can incorporate different seasonings.—*C.V.*

YIELD: 6 TO 8 SERVINGS ⋯•⋯ **ACTIVE TIME: 5 MINUTES** ⋯•⋯ **TOTAL TIME: 1 HOUR**

1 lb. chestnuts

½ teaspoon salt

¼ teaspoon pepper

2 tablespoons unsalted butter, melted

1 tablespoon olive oil

3 sprigs of thyme

1 cinnamon stick

2 whole cloves

1 Preheat the oven to 425°F. Carve an "X" on the rounded side of each chestnut and place in a bowl of hot water. Soak for about 1 minute.

2 Drain the chestnuts and create an aluminum foil pouch. Place the chestnuts in the pouch, sprinkle with salt and pepper, drizzle with the butter and olive oil, and add the thyme, cinnamon stick, and cloves to the pouch. Close the pouch, leaving an opening so that steam can escape.

3 Place in the oven and roast until tender, 40 to 45 minutes. Remove from the oven and serve warm.

CELERY ROOT PUREE

CELERY ROOT, WHICH IS ALSO KNOWN AS CELERIAC, is mildly peppery and very tasty. Whenever I work with it, I remind myself to keep it simple and allow the unique flavor to shine.—*K.S.*

YIELD: 4 SERVINGS ⭍ **ACTIVE TIME: 10 MINUTES** ⭍ **TOTAL TIME: 50 MINUTES**

1½ lbs. celery root

½ cup cream

½ cup milk

Salt and pepper, to taste

1 stick of unsalted butter

1 Trim the ends from the celery root, remove the skin with a vegetable peeler, and use a knife to cut out any recessed or pocked areas. Cut the remainder into thin slices.

2 Place the celery root, cream, milk, salt, and pepper in a saucepan and bring to a simmer over medium heat, while stirring occasionally. Cook until the celery root is fork tender.

3 Transfer the mixture to a blender and puree.

4 Add the butter, season with salt and pepper, and serve.

SHAVED BRUSSELS SPROUTS & KALE SALAD
WITH BLOOD ORANGE VINAIGRETTE

BRUSSELS SPROUTS ARE AS DELICIOUS RAW as they are cooked, and pairing their robust, savory flavor with highly acidic winter citrus is the perfect way to play up that attribute.—*C.V.*

YIELD: 4 TO 6 SERVINGS ⟶ **ACTIVE TIME: 10 MINUTES** ⟶ **TOTAL TIME: 25 MINUTES**

FOR THE VINAIGRETTE

½ cup blood orange juice (about 2 blood oranges)

½ teaspoon salt

¼ teaspoon pepper

1½ tablespoons apple cider vinegar

1 tablespoon honey

1 ice cube
(see page 70 for note on ice cube)

1 cup canola oil

FOR THE SALAD

½ lb. bacon

3 blood oranges, peeled

1 lb. Brussels sprouts, trimmed and sliced thin with a mandoline

2 cups baby kale

Salt and pepper, to taste

½ cup toasted pecans, for garnish

Shaved Parmesan cheese, for garnish

1 Prepare the vinaigrette. Place all of the ingredients, except for the canola oil in a blender. Puree on high and add the canola oil in a slow stream. Puree until the mixture has emulsified and season to taste. Set aside.

2 Place the bacon strips in a sauté pan and cook over medium heat until crisp, about 7 minutes. Transfer to a paper towel–lined plate to drain. When cool enough to handle, chop into bite-sized pieces.

3 Remove the skin from the segments of blood orange and cut each in half. Place in a mixing bowl, add the Brussels sprouts and kale, season with salt and pepper, and toss to combine. Add ⅔ cup of the vinaigrette, toss to evenly coat, and season to taste.

4 Plate the salad, top with the bacon, garnish with the toasted pecans and Parmesan, and serve with the remaining dressing on the side.

ROASTED PORK CHOPS
WITH NEW ENGLAND BAKED BEANS

WITH PORK CHOPS, KEITH AND I WANT TO ENSURE that the quality of the product comes through. By searing it, basting it with a pan sauce, and putting it alongside the sweet richness of baked beans, we're certain that the unmatched flavor of locally raised, heritage pork won't go unnoticed.—*C.V.*

YIELD: 6 SERVINGS ⇢•⇠ **ACTIVE TIME: 1 HOUR AND 15 MINUTES** ⇢•⇠ **TOTAL TIME: 24 HOURS**

1 Drain the beans, place them in a saucepan, and cover with cold water. Bring to a boil, reduce the heat so that the beans simmer, and cook until they are just shy of completely tender, about 1½ hours. Drain, reserve the cooking liquid, and set the beans aside.

2 Preheat the oven to 300°F. Place half of the canola oil and bacon in a saucepan and cook over medium heat until the bacon is crispy. Add the onions, carrots, celery, and garlic and cook until the onions are translucent. Add the beans, 2 cups of the reserved cooking liquid, ketchup, brown sugar, molasses, maple syrup, Worcestershire sauce, and salt and bring to a boil.

3 Transfer to a baking dish, cover with aluminum foil, and place in the oven. Bake until the beans are completely tender, 2 to 2½ hours. If the cooking liquid evaporates while the beans are baking, add more of the reserved cooking liquid as needed. Remove from the oven and season to taste.

4 Allow the pork chops to rest at room temperature for 20 to 30 minutes before cooking.

5 Preheat the oven to 475°F. Place a large cast-iron skillet over high heat, add the remaining canola oil, and season the pork chops with salt and cracked black pepper. Working in batches, place the pork chops in the pan when the oil starts to smoke. Cook for 2 minutes on each side, then use kitchen tongs to flip the pork chops onto their fatty side. Cook until the fat renders and the fatty side is brown.

6 Lay the pork chops flat in the pan, add the butter, thyme, garlic, and shallot. Using a large spoon, baste the pork chops with the pan sauce and cook for another minute before transferring the skillet to the oven. Cook until the internal temperature is 150°F, 5 to 8 minutes depending on thickness. Remove, transfer to a wire rack, and let them rest for 8 to 10 minutes before serving alongside the baked beans.

1 cup cattle beans, soaked overnight
4 tablespoons canola oil
6 oz. bacon, cut into 1-inch pieces
2 cups diced onions
1 cup diced carrots
1 cup diced celery
1 tablespoon chopped garlic
½ cup ketchup
1 cup brown sugar
2 tablespoons molasses
2 tablespoons maple syrup
2 tablespoons Worcestershire sauce
1 tablespoon salt, plus more to taste
6 (10 oz.) pork chops
Cracked black pepper, to taste
2 tablespoons unsalted butter
3 sprigs of thyme
3 garlic cloves
1 shallot, halved

CHICKEN STOCK

YIELD: 8 CUPS · ACTIVE TIME: 20 MINUTES · TOTAL TIME: 6 HOURS

7 lbs. chicken bones, rinsed

½ lb. chicken feet (optional)

4 cups chopped onions

2 cups chopped carrots

2 cups chopped celery

3 garlic cloves, crushed

3 sprigs of thyme

1 teaspoon black peppercorns

1 bay leaf

1   Place the bones and, if using, chicken feet in a large saucepan and cover with cold water. Bring to a simmer over medium-high heat and use a ladle to skim off any impurities that float to the top. Add the vegetables, thyme, peppercorns, and bay leaf, reduce the heat to low, and simmer for 5 hours, while skimming to remove any impurities that rise to the top.

2   Strain, allow to cool slightly, and transfer to the refrigerator. Leave uncovered and allow to cool completely. Remove layer of fat, cover, and store in the refrigerator for 3 to 5 days.

PORK & BEAN STEW

GROWING UP, I ATE A LOT OF STEWS and braised meat dishes. I loved them, but didn't realize what went into getting that flavor. Once I started making them on my own, I learned to appreciate the final result even more.—*C.V.*

YIELD: 4 TO 6 SERVINGS ⇢•⇠ **ACTIVE TIME: 1 HOUR** ⇢•⇠ **TOTAL TIME: 24 HOURS**

1 cup cannellini beans,
soaked overnight

1½-lb. pork shoulder, cut into
1-inch cubes

1½ tablespoons salt

2 teaspoons black pepper

¼ cup all-purpose flour

¼ cup canola oil

2 cups diced onions

1 cup diced celery

1 cup diced carrots

2 cups oyster mushrooms

4 large garlic cloves, minced

3 tablespoons tomato paste

2 cups Chicken Stock (see sidebar)

2 cups Tomato Sauce (see page 198)

4 sprigs of thyme

1 bay leaf

¼ cup chopped parsley leaves,
for garnish

1 Drain the beans, place them in a saucepan, and cover with water. Bring to a boil, reduce heat so that the beans simmer, and cook until tender, about 1 hour. Strain and reserve the cooking liquid. Set the beans aside.

2 Place the pork in a mixing bowl, add the salt and pepper, and toss to coat. Add the flour and toss to coat.

3 Place the canola oil in a Dutch oven and warm over high heat. When the oil starts to smoke, add half of the pork pieces in a single layer and cook until they are browned on all sides. Transfer the seared pieces to a plate, add the remaining pork, and cook until browned all over. Transfer to the plate with the other pork.

4 Place the onions, celery, carrots, mushrooms, and garlic in the pot and cook until onions are translucent. Add the tomato paste and the cannellini beans and stir to coat. Place the pork back in the pot and deglaze with the stock.

5 Add the sauce, thyme, and bay leaf and bring the stew to a boil. Reduce heat so that the stew simmers, cover, and cook, while stirring occasionally, until the stew has thickened to the desired consistency, 35 to 45 minutes. Season to taste, ladle into warmed bowls, and garnish with the parsley.

BUTTERNUT SQUASH & CHORIZO BISQUE

I LOVE TO TASTE the result of pitting sweet against spicy. This toothsome bisque is what came out of one such experiment.—*K.S.*

YIELD: 4 SERVINGS ⇢•⇠ **ACTIVE TIME: 15 MINUTES** ⇢•⇠ **TOTAL TIME: 1 HOUR AND 30 MINUTES**

---

1 large Butternut squash, peeled and sliced

1 onion, sliced

2 tablespoons vegetable oil

Salt and pepper, to taste

1 tablespoon olive oil

½ lb. chorizo, casing removed

2 bay leaves

1 cup heavy cream

1 cup Roasted Vegetable Stock (see page 201)

1 cup milk

4 tablespoons unsalted butter

1 Preheat the oven to 400°F.

2 Place the squash, onion, vegetable oil, and salt in a bowl and toss to combine. Place the mixture in a baking dish and cook until the onion is browned, about 15 to 25 minutes. Transfer the onion to a bowl, return the squash to the oven, and bake for another 20 to 30 minutes, until the squash is fork tender. Remove from the oven and transfer to the bowl containing the onion.

3 Place the olive oil in a skillet and warm over medium-high heat. When the oil is ready, add the chorizo and cook, while turning, until it is browned all over, about 5 minutes. Remove and set on a paper towel–lined plate to drain. When cool enough to handle, chop the chorizo into bite-sized pieces.

4 Place the squash, onion, chorizo, bay leaves, cream, stock, and milk in a large saucepan and bring to a boil over medium-high heat, while stirring often. Reduce heat so that the soup simmers and cook for another 20 minutes.

5 Remove the bay leaves, transfer the soup to a blender, and puree until smooth. Return the soup to the saucepan and bring to a simmer. Add the butter, stir until it has melted, and serve.

CHICKEN BOLOGNESE WITH PENNE

BOLOGNESE IS TRADITIONALLY MADE with ground beef and pork. By substituting ground chicken, you end up with a lighter sauce that allows the other flavors in the dish to shine. As if pasta wasn't enough comfort, using some of the Tomato Sauce you preserved and stashed away will kindle plenty of pleasant memories.—*C.V.*

YIELD: 4 TO 6 SERVINGS ⇢•⇠ **ACTIVE TIME: 45 MINUTES** ⇢•⇠ **TOTAL TIME: 2 HOURS**

2 tablespoons canola oil

½ lb. bacon

1½ lbs. ground chicken

Salt and pepper, to taste

1 cup diced carrots

1 cup diced celery

2 cups diced onions

2 tablespoons minced garlic

1 tablespoon chopped thyme leaves

2 cups Sherry

8 cups Tomato Sauce (see page 198)

1 cup water

1 cup heavy cream

2 tablespoons chopped sage leaves

1 lb. penne

4 tablespoons unsalted butter

1 cup grated Parmesan cheese, plus more for garnish

1 tablespoon chopped basil, for garnish

Red pepper flakes, for garnish (optional)

1 Place the canola oil and bacon in a Dutch oven and cook over high heat until the bacon is crispy. Add the chicken, season with salt and pepper, and cook until it is browned and cooked through. Remove the bacon and the chicken and set aside.

2 Lower the heat to medium and add the carrots, celery, onions, and garlic. Season with salt and cook until the carrots are tender.

3 Return the bacon and chicken to the pan, add the thyme and Sherry, and cook until the wine is nearly evaporated. Add the Tomato Sauce and water, reduce the heat to low, and cook for approximately 45 minutes, while stirring often, until the sauce has thickened.

4 Add the cream and sage and cook for an additional 15 minutes.

5 Bring a large pot of salted water to a boil, add the penne, and cook until just before al dente. Reserve 1 cup of the pasta water, drain the penne, and then return it to the pot. Add the butter, bolognese, and reserved pasta water and stir to combine. Add the Parmesan and stir until melted. Garnish with additional Parmesan, the basil, and red pepper flakes, if desired.

CHICKEN POT PIES

HERE'S THE PERFECT LANDING SPOT for those vegetables you laid away in the freezer to counter your inevitable cravings. Each bite of peas and corn brings with it the sweetness of spring and summer, guaranteeing that these pot pies will brighten the darkest days.—𝓒.𝓥.

YIELD: 8 SERVINGS ⟶ **ACTIVE TIME: 1 HOUR** ⟶ **TOTAL TIME: 2 HOURS AND 45 MINUTES**

1 Preheat the oven to 400°F.

2 Place the chicken breasts in a baking dish and drizzle with the olive oil. Place in the oven and bake until the internal temperature is 160°F, about 15 to 20 minutes. Remove and let cool. When cool enough to handle, cut the chicken into bite-sized cubes. Lower the oven temperature to 375°F.

3 Place the butter, carrots, celery, and onions in a large pot and cook over medium-high heat until the onions turn translucent. Place the stock in a separate saucepan and warm over medium-high heat.

4 Add the flour to the vegetable mixture and cook, while stirring constantly, until the mixture gives off a nutty aroma, about 2 minutes. Pour the warmed stock into the pan while stirring to prevent lumps from forming. When the stock has been incorporated and the mixture is smooth, add the chicken, corn, and peas. Cook for 2 minutes and then remove from heat.

5 Prepare the piecrusts. Place the flour, 2 teaspoons of the salt, pepper, parsley, and thyme in a large mixing bowl and stir to combine. Divide the butter into tablespoons and place them in the freezer for 15 minutes.

6 Place the flour mixture and the butter in a food processor and pulse 4 to 5 times. Slowly pour the 1 cup of ice-cold water into the food processor and pulse until the mixture is just combined.

7 Transfer the dough to a lightly floured work surface and knead until it is smooth. Place the dough in the refrigerator for at least 20 minutes.

8 Remove the dough from the fridge and divide it into 16 pieces. Roll each piece to a thickness of ⅛ inch. Place one crust in eight different miniature cast-iron skillets or au gratin dishes, making sure that the crust extends over the sides. Prick the crusts with a fork, cover each with a piece of parchment paper, and fill the crusts with uncooked rice. Place in the oven and bake for 15 minutes. Remove, discard the rice, and fill each crust with some of the chicken-and-vegetable mixture.

9 Lay another crust over the top and crimp the edges. Place the 2 teaspoons of water, egg yolk, and salt in a bowl and beat to combine. Cut a slit in the top crust and then brush it with the egg wash. Place the pies on a baking sheet, place them in the oven, and bake until the top crust is golden brown, 35 to 40 minutes. Remove from the oven and let cool slightly before serving.

FOR THE FILLING

6 (4 oz.) chicken breasts

3 tablespoons olive oil

1 stick of unsalted butter

1 cup diced carrots

1 cup diced celery

2 cups diced onions

5 cups Chicken Stock (see page 236)

¾ cup all-purpose flour

1 cup frozen corn

1 cup frozen peas

FOR THE PIECRUSTS

5 cups all-purpose flour, plus more for dusting

2½ teaspoons salt

1 teaspoon pepper

2 tablespoons chopped parsley leaves

1 tablespoon chopped thyme leaves

4 sticks of unsalted butter

1 cup ice-cold water, plus 2 teaspoons

Uncooked rice, as needed

1 egg yolk

CHICKEN & ROOT VEGETABLE STEW

SINCE YOU CAN STILL FIND a few locally grown root vegetables during the wintertime, we created this stew to provide them with a worthy home. The wonderful thing about this hearty stew—other than the taste—is that it can facilitate almost any substitution, so long as you have a great stock supplying your foundation.—*K.S.*

YIELD: 12 SERVINGS ⟶ **ACTIVE TIME: 20 MINUTES** ⟶ **TOTAL TIME: 2 HOURS AND 30 MINUTES**

1 lb. cooked chicken, shredded

8 cups Chicken Stock (see page 236)

1 lb. celery root

1 lb. potatoes

1 lb. rutabaga

3 sprigs of thyme

3 sprigs of rosemary

4 bay leaves

4 cups water, plus 4 tablespoons

2 large onions, sliced

Salt and pepper, to taste

4 tablespoons cornstarch

1 Place all of the ingredients, except for the cornstarch and the 4 tablespoons of water, in a large pot. Bring to a boil over medium-high heat and then reduce heat so that the stew simmers.

2 Simmer until the liquid has reduced by at least one-third. This should take approximately 2 hours.

3 Place the cornstarch and 4 tablespoons of water in a small bowl and stir until well combined. Add the mixture to the stew and stir until it has thickened.

4 Remove the sprigs of thyme and rosemary, season with salt and pepper, and ladle into warmed bowls.

CELERY ROOT BISQUE WITH
POACHED CLAMS & PARSLEY OIL

CLAMS, WHICH BECOME SWEETER in the late fall and early winter, are a natural for this rich, creamy bisque that celery root forms the base of. The key to this dish is using the poaching liquid in the soup, as it bridges the gap between the flavors.—*C.V.*

YIELD: 4 TO 6 SERVINGS ⇢• **ACTIVE TIME: 40 MINUTES** ⇢• **TOTAL TIME: 3 HOURS**

---

18 littleneck clams

2½ tablespoons salt, plus more to taste

1 cup white wine

2 shallots, sliced

6 garlic cloves, 3 crushed, 3 sliced

6 sprigs of thyme

2 bay leaves

4 tablespoons unsalted butter

1 yellow onion, sliced

1 cup sliced celery

8 cups peeled and diced celery root

2 cups heavy cream

6 cups whole milk

1 cup parsley leaves

⅓ cup canola oil

1 Place the clams and 1 tablespoon of the salt in a large pot and cover with cold water. Soak for 2 hours to remove some of the sand from the clams, making sure to change the water every 30 minutes.

2 Drain the clams, place them in a large pot, and add the white wine, the shallots, the crushed garlic cloves, 4 sprigs of thyme, and 1 of the bay leaves. Cover and cook over high heat until the majority of the clams have opened. Discard any clams that do not open. Strain and reserve 1½ cups of the cooking liquid. Remove the clam meat from the shells and set aside.

3 Place the butter, onion, celery, and sliced garlic in a large pot and cook over medium-high heat until the onion is translucent. Add the celery root, cream, milk, remaining salt, remaining bay leaf, remaining thyme, and reserved cooking liquid and simmer over low heat until the celery root is tender, about 20 minutes.

4 Remove the sprigs of thyme and bay leaf, transfer the bisque to a blender, and puree until smooth. Return to the saucepan, season to taste, and add the clam meat. Simmer over low heat until the clam meat is warmed through, about 2 minutes.

5 Place the parsley leaves and canola oil in a blender and puree on high, about 1 minute. Strain the oil through a piece of cheesecloth or a coffee filter and discard the solids. This oil can be stored in the refrigerator for up to 1 week.

6 Ladle the soup into bowls, garnish with the parsley oil, and serve.

BOILED DINNER

ANOTHER DISH MADE ICONIC by the people of New England. It can be prepared with corned beef or ham, though I tend to lean toward ham when I prepare it. The leftovers make for amazing sandwiches, so make sure you reserve a little for the next day.—*K.S.*

YIELD: 6 TO 8 SERVINGS ⇢•⇠ **ACTIVE TIME: 30 MINUTES** ⇢•⇠ **TOTAL TIME: 2 HOURS AND 45 MINUTES**

5- to 6-lb. ham

1 head of cabbage, cut into 6 wedges

6 carrots

6 potatoes

3 bay leaves

1 tablespoon peppercorns

1 large onion, quartered

Whole grain mustard, for serving (optional)

Horseradish, for serving (optional)

1 Place all of the ingredients, aside from those designated for serving, in a large pot and cover with water.

2 Bring to a boil over medium-high heat. Cover, reduce heat so that the water simmers, and cook until the ham and vegetables are tender, about 2½ hours.

3 Remove the vegetables and ham from the water, transfer to a carving board, and allow to cool for 10 to 15 minutes.

4 Cut the ham and vegetables to desired size. If desired, serve with whole grain mustard or horseradish.

BLACK FOREST TRIFLE WITH
PRESERVED CHERRIES & COCOA CRUMBLE

BEFORE I HAD ANY DESIGNS on a culinary career, making trifle for family gatherings was something that always made me happy. A trip to Enna Chocolate in Epping, New Hampshire, had me eager to use chocolate everywhere I could, including in this mature spin on my childhood favorite.—*C.V.*

YIELD: 10 TO 12 SERVINGS ⸰⸱⸰ **ACTIVE TIME: 45 MINUTES** ⸰⸱⸰ **TOTAL TIME: 8 HOURS**

1 Preheat the oven to 350°F and grease a round 9" cake pan.

2 Place the eggs and sugar in the bowl of a stand mixer fitted with the whisk attachment and beat on medium until pale and fluffy. Add the butter, sour cream, orange zest, and half of the cherry liqueur and beat until combined.

3 Sift the flours, cocoa powder, baking powder, baking soda, and salt into a bowl. Add the dry mixture to the batter and beat until just combined. Scrape the bowl as needed while mixing the batter.

4 Pour the batter into the prepared pan, place it in the oven, and bake for 20 to 25 minutes, until a toothpick inserted into the center comes out clean. Remove from the oven and let cool in the pan for 10 minutes before transferring to a wire rack to cool completely. Keep the oven at 350°F.

5 Place the cherries and the remaining liqueur in a bowl and let sit for at least 30 minutes. Strain, set the cherries aside, and combine the liquid with the water. Set aside.

6 Prepare the crumble. Sift the sugar, flour, and cocoa powder into a bowl. Add the melted butter and work the mixture with a fork until it is crumbly. Place the mixture on a parchment–lined baking sheet in an even layer, place it in the oven, and bake until crunchy, about 25 minutes. Remove from the oven and let cool completely.

7 Prepare the whipped cream. Place the heavy cream, confectioners' sugar, salt, and liqueur in a mixing bowl and whip until stiff peaks form.

8 When you are ready to assemble the trifle, cut the cake into 1½-inch pieces. Cover the bottom of a 3-quart trifle bowl with pieces of cake, breaking pieces as needed to fill up any empty space. Brush the pieces of cake with the reserved liqueur-and-water mixture. Top with layers of whipped cream, cherries, and cocoa crumble. Repeat this layering process two more times. Top the trifle with a layer of whipped cream and sprinkle any remaining cherries and crumble on top.

FOR THE CAKE

3 eggs

⅔ cup sugar

4 tablespoons unsalted butter, melted

¼ cup sour cream

½ teaspoon orange zest

4 tablespoons cherry liqueur

⅔ cup cake flour

⅓ cup all-purpose flour

½ cup cocoa powder

1 teaspoon baking powder

¼ teaspoon baking soda

1½ teaspoons salt

2 cups Preserved Cherries (see sidebar), quartered

¼ cup water

FOR THE COCOA CRUMBLE

1 cup confectioners' sugar

⅔ cup all-purpose flour

½ cup cocoa powder

1 stick of unsalted butter, melted

FOR THE WHIPPED CREAM

1 cup heavy cream

2 tablespoons confectioners' sugar

½ teaspoon salt

1 tablespoon cherry liqueur

PRESERVED CHERRIES

**YIELD: 2 CUPS · ACTIVE TIME: 15 MINUTES
TOTAL TIME: 6½ HOURS**

2 cups cherries (or any stone fruit)

2 cups sugar

1 cup water

¼ cup lemon juice

1 Wash the cherries thoroughly and then remove the pits and stems.

2 Place the sugar, water, and lemon juice in a saucepan and bring to a boil over medium-high heat. Cook, while stirring, until the sugar is dissolved. Remove from heat and let cool for 5 minutes.

3 Place the cherries in sterilized mason jars and cover with the syrup. Can according to the instructions on page 271.

CAFÉ MOCHA

GROWING UP, MY DAD ALWAYS MADE HOT CHOCOLATE using pure cocoa from Haiti, a rich and creamy treat that was a source of comfort when winter started to drag. This version is equally soothing, so don't hesitate to wow the crowd with it at a holiday gathering. Special thanks to Ogusky Ceramics & Design Studio in Boston for this wonderful mug. —*C.V.*

YIELD: 10 CUPS ···· ACTIVE TIME: 10 MINUTES ···· TOTAL TIME: 20 MINUTES

8 cups whole milk

1 cup heavy cream

½ cup sugar, plus more to taste

4 oz. espresso

½ lb. bittersweet chocolate, chopped

1 tablespoon orange zest

½ teaspoon salt

1 Place the milk, cream, sugar, and espresso in a saucepan and warm over medium heat.

2 Place the chocolate in a bowl. When the milk mixture is hot, ladle 1 cup into the bowl containing the chocolate and whisk until the chocolate is completely melted, adding more of the warm milk mixture if the melted chocolate mixture is too thick.

3 Pour the melted chocolate mixture into the pot and whisk to combine. Add the orange zest and salt, stir to combine, and adjust to taste before serving.

GINGERBREAD MADELEINES

THE HUNT FOR SWEET TREATS NEVER STOPS around Christmas time, and this seasonal take on one of my favorite French pastries, the madeleine, has the potential to become a beloved tradition in your home.—*E.V.*

YIELD: 16 MADELEINES ⋯► **ACTIVE TIME: 25 MINUTES** ⋯► **TOTAL TIME: 3 HOURS**

5 tablespoons unsalted butter, plus more for the pan

½ cup brown sugar

2 eggs

1 tablespoon minced ginger

1¼ teaspoons vanilla extract

1½ tablespoons molasses

⅓ cup whole milk

½ cup all-purpose flour

½ cup cake flour

¼ teaspoon baking powder

1½ teaspoons salt

¼ teaspoon ground cloves

¼ teaspoon nutmeg

1 teaspoon cinnamon

1 Place the butter in a small saucepan and cook over medium heat until lightly brown. Remove from heat and let cool to room temperature.

2 Place the butter and the brown sugar in the bowl of a stand mixer fitted with the whisk attachment. Beat on high until light and frothy. Lower the speed, add the eggs one at a time, and beat until incorporated. Add the ginger, vanilla, molasses, and milk and beat until incorporated.

3 Sift the flours and baking powder into a bowl. Add the salt, cloves, nutmeg, and cinnamon and stir to combine.

4 Gradually add the dry mixture to the wet mixture and beat until the dry mixture has been thoroughly incorporated. Transfer the dough to the refrigerator and chill for 2 hours.

5 Preheat the oven to 375°F and brush each shell-shaped depression in the madeleine pan with butter. Place the pan in the freezer for at least 10 minutes.

6 Remove the pan from the freezer and the batter from the refrigerator. Fill each "shell" two-thirds of the way with batter, place the pan in the oven, and bake until a toothpick inserted into the center of a cookie comes out clean, about 12 minutes. Remove from the oven and place the cookies on a wire rack to cool slightly. Serve warm or at room temperature.

GINGERBREAD ICE CREAM

SOME PEOPLE BUILD HOUSES WITH GINGERBREAD, we make ice cream. If you decide to follow our tack, be careful—this is incredibly addictive.—*K.S.*

YIELD: 6 SERVINGS ⋯► **ACTIVE TIME: 30 MINUTES** ⋯► **TOTAL TIME: 14 TO 32 HOURS**

1½ cups heavy cream

1½ cups whole milk

2 teaspoons ground ginger

2 teaspoons cinnamon

1 teaspoon nutmeg

¼ teaspoon ground cloves

2 tablespoons molasses

Pinch of salt

⅔ cup sugar

5 egg yolks

1 Place all of the ingredients, except for the sugar and egg yolks, in a medium saucepan and cook over medium heat until the mixture starts to bubble.

2 Remove from heat and allow the mixture to steep for 30 minutes to 1 hour.

3 Strain, discard the solids, wipe out the saucepan, and return the liquid to it. Bring to a simmer over medium heat.

4 Place the sugar and egg yolks in a bowl and whisk until combined. Add a little bit of the mixture in the saucepan to the eggs, stirring to keep from cooking the eggs.

5 Add the tempered eggs to the saucepan and cook until the mixture is thick enough to coat the back of a wooden spoon. Remove from heat and let cool. Cover the pan and transfer to the refrigerator for 6 to 24 hours.

6 When you are ready to make the ice cream, place the mixture in your ice cream maker and churn until the desired texture is achieved. Freeze for at least 6 hours before serving.

SQUASH WHOOPIE PIES WITH GINGER CREAM

THE WHOOPIE PIE IS AN INCREDIBLE DESSERT that, for whatever reason, remains largely within the boundaries of New England. It's typically made with chocolate, but I've found that these sweet treats are even more delicious using some of the autumn squash that I've laid away.—*K.S.*

YIELD: 12 SERVINGS ⇥ **ACTIVE TIME: 20 MINUTES** ⇥ **TOTAL TIME: 1 HOUR**

1⅓ cups all-purpose flour

1 teaspoon cinnamon

1 teaspoon ground ginger

¼ teaspoon ground cloves

½ teaspoon nutmeg

½ teaspoon baking soda

½ teaspoon baking powder

1 teaspoon salt

1 cup light brown sugar

2 tablespoons maple syrup

1 cup pureed Butternut or Acorn squash

1 egg

1 cup vegetable oil

1⅓ cups powdered sugar

4 tablespoons unsalted butter

1 cup cream cheese

2 teaspoons grated fresh ginger

½ teaspoon vanilla extract

1 Preheat the oven to 350°F. Sift the flour, cinnamon, ground ginger, cloves, nutmeg, baking soda, baking powder, and salt into a mixing bowl.

2 Place the brown sugar, maple syrup, pureed squash, egg, and vegetable oil in a separate mixing bowl and stir until combined. Sift the dry mixture into the squash mixture and stir until it has been incorporated.

3 Use an ice cream scoop to place dollops of the batter onto a greased baking sheet. Make sure to leave plenty of space between the scoops. Place the sheet in the oven and bake until golden brown, about 10 to 15 minutes. Remove and let cool.

4 While the squash cakes are cooling, place the remaining ingredients in a bowl and beat until combined and fluffy.

5 When the cakes have cooled completely, spread the powdered sugar-and-butter filling on one of the cakes. Top with another cake and repeat until all of the cakes and filling have been used.

CARROT CAKE

WHILE POKING AROUND MY FREEZER one frigid day, I came across a bag of carrot peels that I'd stowed away. Since the winter is the time when I like to bake, I used them in this carrot cake, which is moist and delicious.—*K.S.*

YIELD: 8 TO 10 SERVINGS ⟶ **ACTIVE TIME: 20 MINUTES** ⟶ **TOTAL TIME: 2 HOURS AND 15 MINUTES**

2 cups shredded carrots

2 cups sugar

1½ cups all-purpose flour

1½ tablespoons baking soda

1 teaspoon salt

1 tablespoon cinnamon

3 eggs

1¾ cups vegetable oil

2 teaspoons vanilla extract

½ cup chopped walnuts (optional)

1 Preheat the oven to 350°F.

2 Place the carrots and sugar in a mixing bowl, stir to combine, and let the mixture sit for 10 minutes.

3 Place the flour, baking soda, salt, and cinnamon in a mixing bowl and stir to combine. Place the eggs, vegetable oil, and vanilla extract in a separate mixing bowl and stir to combine. Add the wet mixture to the dry mixture and stir until the mixture is a smooth batter. Stir in the carrots and, if desired, the walnuts.

4 Transfer the batter to a greased 9" cake pan and place the cake in the oven. Bake until the top is browned and a knife inserted into the center comes out clean, about 40 to 50 minutes.

5 Remove the cake from the oven, transfer to a wire rack, and let cool for 1 hour before slicing.

LEAF LARD PIECRUST

LEAF LARD IS THE HIGHEST GRADE OF LARD, coming from the visceral fat around a pig's kidneys and loin. Spreadable at room temperature, it is the perfect base for a flaky, flavorful piecrust.—*K.S.*

YIELD: 9-INCH PIECRUSTS ⇢ **ACTIVE TIME: 12 MINUTES** ⇢ **TOTAL TIME: 2 HOURS**

2½ cups all-purpose flour

1½ tablespoons sugar

1 teaspoon salt

6 oz. cold leaf lard, cubed

2 tablespoons cold unsalted butter, cubed

5 tablespoons ice-cold water, plus more as needed

1   Place the flour, sugar, and salt in a bowl and stir until combined.

2   Add the lard and butter and use a pastry blender to work them into the flour mixture. Work the mixture until it is a coarse meal, making sure to smooth out any large chunks.

3   Add the water and continue to work the mixture until it is a smooth dough. If it feels too dry, add more water in 1-teaspoon increments. Form the dough into a large ball and then cut it in half. Wrap each piece in plastic wrap and place in the refrigerator for 2 hours before using. The dough will keep in the refrigerator for up to 3 days. It also freezes very well, and can be stored in a freezer for 3 to 6 months.

PRESERVATION & FERMENTATION

· KIMCHI TO KOMBUCHA ·

WHEN SEASONS change as dramatically as they do in New England, it is essential to find ways to hold on to the gifts of a season.

When it comes to preservation, we cannot stress safety enough. Having a clean and sterile work surface along with properly vetted techniques will keep you and your family safe to enjoy these wonderful preservation methods.

We became enamored with preservation after meeting our friend Jitti Chaithiraphant. He is somewhat of a legend in the Boston area for his unbelievable knowledge of fermentation and foraging. We spent some time learning about proper methods of fermentation from him, tasting vinegars for hours and fostering an appreciation for how fermentation affects our everyday lives. One day, we left Jitti's house and knew that we had to explore the realm of preservation.

Along our journey we've learned from amazing people like William Dunkerley of Dunk's Mushrooms. Dunk taught us how to identify various species of mushrooms, forage for wild edibles, and turn fermented wild spruce tips into unbelievable syrup. Jitti and Dunk changed our approach to food by uncovering an entirely different path to wander down. Soon we found ourselves making kombucha, syrups from wild ingredients, and foraged kimchi. Once we understood how to properly can, pickle, and ferment, we stopped thinking about a course in terms of starch, protein, and vegetable and began wondering how the sour tang of fermented foods could accent pork belly. We would share ideas and recipes and soon found ourselves with rooms full of gently bubbling mason jars.

For us, capturing a season through preservation is like opening a time capsule. Popping that jar of fresh summer tomatoes on a cold winter night and making a sauce has special meaning. You remember the act of canning, you remember where the ingredients came from, and you appreciate the work that went into it.

◆ ● ◆

CANNING 101

PROPER CANNING ALLOWS YOU to preserve the best aspects of each season. This time-honored tradition is simple, but it is important to follow each and every step. Once you get the hang of it, you will be canning everything in sight.

Mason jars with lids and bands

1 large canning pot

1 pair of canning tongs

1 Bring a pot of water to a boil. Place the mason jars in the water for 15 to 20 minutes to sterilize them. Do not boil the mason jar lids, as this may prevent them from creating a proper seal when the time comes.

2 Bring water to a boil in the large canning pot.

3 Fill the sterilized mason jars with whatever you are canning. Place the lids on the jars and secure the bands tightly. Place the jars in the boiling water for 40 minutes.

4 Use the tongs to remove the jars from the boiling water and let them cool. As they are cooling, you should hear the classic "ping and pop" sound of the lids creating a seal.

5 After 4 to 6 hours, check the lids. There should be no give in them and they should be suctioned onto the jars. Discard any lids and food that did not seal properly.

MIXED BERRY JAM

THANKS TO THIS JAM, the brief glory of berry season in New England can be savored all year long.—*C.V.*

YIELD: 2½ CUPS ⋯•⋯ **ACTIVE TIME: 10 MINUTES** ⋯•⋯ **TOTAL TIME: 1 HOUR AND 30 MINUTES**

6 cups strawberries, hulled, cored, and quartered

2 cups blueberries

2 cups raspberries

½ cup sugar

1¼ tablespoons pectin

1 Place the berries and sugar in a large saucepan and cook, while stirring, over medium-high heat. When the sugar has dissolved and the berries start breaking down and releasing their liquid, reduce the heat to medium and cook, while stirring every 10 minutes, until the berries are very soft and the mixture has thickened, 30 to 40 minutes.

2 While stirring, sprinkle the pectin onto the mixture and cook for another minute until the berries are soft.

3 Transfer the jam to sterilized mason jars and can according to the instructions on page 271.

NOTE: If you don't want to go through the canning process, simply allow the jam to cool completely in the mason jars before applying the lids. The jam will keep in the refrigerator for 1 week.

ROSEMARY SIMPLE SYRUP

SIMPLE SYRUPS SERVE MANY DIFFERENT FUNCTIONS. Not only do they lend themselves to cocktails, they also work very well in desserts. Because of this versatility, I always have some on hand. Feel free to experiment with any herb or fruit in place of the rosemary. —*K.S.*

YIELD: 1½ CUPS ⟶ **ACTIVE TIME: 10 MINUTES** ⟶ **TOTAL TIME: 1 HOUR AND 15 MINUTES**

4 sprigs of rosemary

1 cup sugar

1 cup water

1 Place the ingredients in a medium saucepan and bring the mixture to a boil over medium heat. Reduce the heat to low and allow the mixture to simmer for 10 minutes.

2 Remove the pan from heat and let the mixture stand for 1 to 2 hours. Remove the sprigs of rosemary, transfer the mixture to a mason jar, cover, and store in the refrigerator for up to 1 month.

HOT HONEY

THIS IS ONE OF OUR FAVORITE WAYS to spice up a dessert menu. The touch of heat amidst all that sweet is a surprise that goes down well every time. You can also drizzle it over yogurt in the morning to kick-start your day. —*K.S.*

YIELD: 1 CUP ⋯•⋯ **ACTIVE TIME: 10 MINUTES** ⋯•⋯ **TOTAL TIME: 2 HOURS**

---

4 hot chili peppers

1 cup honey

1 Place the chili peppers and honey in a saucepan and bring to a very gentle simmer over medium-low heat. Reduce heat to lowest possible setting and cook for 1 hour.

2 Remove the saucepan from heat and let the mixture infuse for another hour.

3 Remove the peppers. Transfer the honey to a container, cover, and store in the refrigerator.

NOTE: We've found that Fresno and cayenne peppers produce the best results. If you're after additional heat, use habanero peppers.

KIMCHI

I HAVE A GOOD FRIEND NAMED CODY TAMAIAN; he is a fantastic potter. I commissioned him to make some fermenting jars for me a little while back, and the first thing I put in them was kimchi. Simple and versatile, it's the perfect introduction to all that fermentation has to offer.—*K.S.*

YIELD: 4 CUPS ⋯ **ACTIVE TIME: 30 MINUTES** ⋯ **TOTAL TIME: 3 TO 7 DAYS**

1 head of Napa cabbage, cut into strips

½ cup salt

2 tablespoons minced ginger

2 tablespoons minced garlic

1 teaspoon sugar

5 tablespoons red pepper flakes

3 bunches of scallions, sliced (whites and greens)

Filtered water, as needed

1 Place the cabbage and salt in a large bowl and stir to combine. Wash your hands, or put on gloves, and work the mixture with your hands, squeezing to remove any liquid from the cabbage. Let the mixture rest for 2 hours.

2 Add the remaining ingredients, work the mixture until well combined, and squeeze to remove any liquid.

3 Transfer the mixture to a container and press down so it is tightly packed together. The liquid should be covering the mixture. If it is not, add water until the mixture is covered.

4 Cover the jar and let the mixture sit at room temperature for 3 to 7 days, removing the lid daily to release the gas that has built up.

FERMENTED HOT SAUCE

HOT SAUCE IS AN ADDICTION OF MINE. Fermented hot sauce took that addiction to the next level. I always have a bottle of this by my side.—*K.S.*

YIELD: 2 CUPS ⋯⋯ **ACTIVE TIME: 10 MINUTES** ⋯⋯ **TOTAL TIME: 30 DAYS TO 6 MONTHS**

2 lbs. cayenne peppers

1 lb. jalapeño peppers

5 garlic cloves

1 red onion, quartered

3 tablespoons salt, plus more to taste

Filtered water, as needed

1 Remove the tops of the peppers and split them down the middle.

2 Place the split peppers and the garlic, onion, and salt in a mason jar and cover with the water. Cover the jar and shake well.

3 Place the jar away from direct sunlight and let stand for a minimum of 30 days, and up to 6 months. Based on my own experience, a longer fermenting time is very much worth it.

4 Once you are ready to make the sauce, reserve most of the brine, transfer the mixture to a blender, and puree to desired thickness. If you want your sauce to be on the thin side, keep adding brine until you have the consistency you want. Season with salt, transfer to a container, cover, and store in the refrigerator for up to 3 months.

SPICY PICKLES

WHEN CUCUMBERS SHOW UP IN THE SPRING, I make a year's supply of these delightful pickles.—*K.S.*

YIELD: 12 CUPS •⊶• **ACTIVE TIME: 20 MINUTES** •⊶• **TOTAL TIME: 5 TO 8 HOURS**

---

3 lbs. pickling cucumbers, sliced thin

3 small yellow onions, sliced thin

1 red bell pepper, cored, seeded, and sliced thin

2 habanero peppers, cored, seeded, and sliced thin

3 garlic cloves, sliced

3 cups sugar

3 cups apple cider vinegar

2 tablespoons mustard seeds

2 teaspoons turmeric

1 teaspoon ground black pepper

⅓ cup canning & pickling salt

1 Place the cucumbers, onions, peppers, and garlic in a large bowl.

2 Place the sugar, apple cider vinegar, mustard seeds, turmeric, and black pepper in a large pot and bring to a boil over medium-high heat, while stirring to dissolve the sugar.

3 Add the vegetables and the salt and return to a boil. Remove the pot from heat and let it cool slightly.

4 Fill sterilized mason jars with the vegetables and cover with the brine. Can according to the instructions on page 271.

PIKLIZ

GROWING UP, I NEVER thought much about this spicy, pickled vegetable slaw that is a staple in Haitian households. I just knew that it was always in the fridge. It wasn't until I started making it for friends that I realized how special the flavors are to me. Serve it with beef or seafood or spread on a sandwich in need of some zip. —*C.V.*

YIELD: 4 CUPS ••• **ACTIVE TIME: 15 MINUTES** ••• **TOTAL TIME: 24 HOURS**

---

4 habanero peppers, seeded and sliced

½ cup sliced cabbage

¼ cup shredded carrot

¼ cup chopped green beans

¼ cup sliced red bell pepper

½ cup sliced shallots

½ cup sliced white onion

White vinegar, as needed

1 Place the vegetables in a large mixing bowl and toss to combine.

2 Transfer the mixture to a large, sterilized mason jar and press down on it. Add vinegar until the mixture is completely covered.

3 If preserving, can according to the instructions on page 271. Otherwise, cover with a lid and let the mixture sit for 1 day before using.

GROWING A SCOBY

A SCOBY is essential to making kombucha. You can buy one online, get one from a friend, or grow one from store-bought kombucha. If you opt for the latter route, this is the easiest method. Just make sure you opt for high-quality kombucha.

YIELD: 1 SCOBY · ACTIVE TIME: 10 MINUTES
TOTAL TIME: 7 TO 30 DAYS

1 cup hot black tea (120°F)
2 tablespoons sugar
1 bottle of raw, unfiltered, unflavored kombucha

1   Combine the tea and sugar and stir until the sugar is dissolved. Let the mixture rest until it is at room temperature.

2   Place the tea and kombucha in a large glass container. Cover with a cloth and secure with a rubber band or kitchen twine. Place the jar away from direct sunlight and let rest at room temperature.

3   A cloudy SCOBY will begin to form after 5 to 7 days. After approximately 2 weeks, you will see the SCOBY start to develop fully. When it resembles a Frisbee, you are ready to start making kombucha.

NOTE: As time goes on, the SCOBY will continue to produce "babies" and thicken. Feel free to peel off layers of it and give them to friends who are interested in making their own kombucha.

KOMBUCHA

KOMBUCHA IS FERMENTED TEA that provides the digestive system with helpful probiotics. And of late, you can find it all over. The process starts with brewing tea and placing it in a jar with a SCOBY (an acronym for symbiotic culture of bacteria and yeast), which aids in the fermentation process. If you're interested in making your own and the endless flavor opportunities this will provide, this recipe is all you need to get started.—*K.S.*

YIELD: 8 CUPS ⋯ **ACTIVE TIME: 20 MINUTES** ⋯ **TOTAL TIME: 1 TO 2 WEEKS**

4 cups filtered water

6 tea bags

1 cup sugar

1 SCOBY (see sidebar)

1 Bring the water to a boil in a saucepan and then remove it from heat.

2 Add the tea bags and sugar and stir to combine. Let stand until cool.

3 When the tea is cooled, transfer it to a jar, add the SCOBY, and cover with a cloth. Place the jar out of direct sunlight and let it sit at room temperature for 1 to 2 weeks. Taste the mixture periodically during the resting period. When the kombucha is ready, it should have a slightly acidic, sour taste with some back-end sweetness.

4 Once you have the desired taste, place fruit and/or additional flavorings into a smaller mason jar. Fill the jar with kombucha, while making sure to leave 2" to 3" of open space at the top of the mason jar.

5 Cover the jar tightly and let stand for 2 days. Open the jar carefully, as the kombucha is likely to be very fizzy.

NOTE: When the kombucha has finished fermenting, keep some of the liquid in the jar with the SCOBY. It will dry out otherwise.

APPLE CIDER VINEGAR

FOOD PREP DOESN'T GET ANY EASIER than making apple cider vinegar. Not only is it delicious, it also prevents waste by using up the apple peels and cores that would otherwise be discarded. Just store the scraps in resealable bags in your freezer until you have enough to make this vinegar. —*K.S.*

YIELD: 2 CUPS ⋯•⋯ **ACTIVE TIME: 10 MINUTES** ⋯•⋯ **TOTAL TIME: 55 TO 65 DAYS**

4 cups apple scraps (peels, cores, and trimmings)

3 tablespoons organic cane sugar

3 cups filtered water, plus more as needed

1 Fill a large mason jar three-quarters of the way with the apple scraps.

2 Place the sugar and water in a bowl and stir until the sugar has dissolved.

3 Pour the mixture into the mason jar, making sure the liquid covers the apple scraps. If necessary, weigh the apple scraps down with a fermentation stone or a cup.

4 Cover the mason jar with cheesecloth and secure with a rubber band or kitchen twine.

5 Place away from direct sunlight and store at room temperature for 5 weeks, checking periodically to make sure the apple scraps are covered by liquid. If more liquid is needed, add water to cover.

6 After 5 weeks, strain out the apple scraps and return the liquid to the mason jar. Cover, place away from direct sunlight, and let the mixture sit for another 20 to 30 days.

CULTURED BUTTER

MIXING CREAM WITH YOGURT and allowing it to ferment for a short time gives it a sweet-and-sour tinge that only amplifies the buttery flavor that we all crave. Intrigued? Give it a try. We bet you never go back to regular old butter on your bread.—*K.S.*

YIELD: 2 CUPS ⸱⸱⸱ **ACTIVE TIME: 10 MINUTES** ⸱⸱⸱ **TOTAL TIME: 3 DAYS**

4 cups high-quality heavy cream

½ cup whole milk yogurt (see page 290 for Homemade Yogurt recipe)

½ teaspoon salt

1 Place the heavy cream and yogurt in a jar. Seal it and shake vigorously.

2 Open the jar, cover with cheesecloth, and secure with a rubber band or kitchen twine.

3 Place the mixture away from direct sunlight and let it sit at room temperature for 36 hours.

4 After 36 hours, seal the jar and place it in the refrigerator for 4 to 6 hours.

5 Remove the mixture from the refrigerator and pour into a mixer. Whip on high, covering with a towel to prevent spilling, until the butter separates from the buttermilk. Reserve the buttermilk for another preparation.

6 Transfer the butter to a cheesecloth and squeeze out any excess liquid. Wash the butter under ice-cold water and store in an airtight container. It will keep in the refrigerator for approximately 3 months.

HOMEMADE YOGURT

THE BEST THING ABOUT MAKING YOUR OWN YOGURT is gaining control over the flavor, and what goes in it. That way you can be certain that it's good for you. This recipe is so basic that even complete novices will have fresh, tangy yogurt in no time.—*K.S.*

YIELD: 8 CUPS ⋅•⋅ ACTIVE TIME: 10 MINUTES ⋅•⋅ TOTAL TIME: 5 HOURS

8 cups whole milk

½ cup store-bought yogurt with active cultures (organic yogurt preferred)

1 Place the milk in a large saucepan and warm, while stirring frequently, until the milk is approximately 200°F. Make sure that the milk does not come to a boil, as it will change the protein structure.

2 Remove the milk from heat and let it cool to 112°F to 115°F, stirring occasionally to prevent a skin from forming.

3 Whisk the milk. Add the store-bought yogurt and continue to whisk. When the temperature is 110°F, place mixture in an insulated thermos, maintaining a temperature of 110°F.

4 After 4 hours, the yogurt will be set. If you prefer a thicker yogurt, keep it in the thermos until the desired consistency has been achieved. Transfer to a container, cover, and allow to cool completely.

SOURDOUGH STARTER

THE SUCCESS OF ANY SOURDOUGH LOAF lies in the quality of the starter, aka levain. While that's a lot of pressure, all you need to handle it is time—the longer the starter has to develop, the more flavor it will impart to the bread.—*K.S.*

YIELD: APPROXIMATELY 100 GRAMS ⇥ **ACTIVE TIME: 1 HOUR** ⇥ **TOTAL TIME: 1 WEEK**

---

1 cup organic rye flour

7 cups water

6 cups bread flour

1 Combine the rye flour and 1 cup of the water in a large mason jar or bowl and stir until thoroughly combined. Put in a dark, naturally warm place and let stand for 24 hours.

2 The next day, discard three-quarters of the mixture. Add 1 cup of the water and 1 cup of the bread flour and stir until thoroughly combined. Let stand for 24 hours.

3 Repeat Step 2 for another 5 days. On the fourth or fifth day, the mixture should start to bubble.

4 After 1 week, you will have a viable sourdough starter. Store the starter in the refrigerator and feed it with 1 cup water and 1 cup bread flour if you will not be making bread during a particular week. When you are ready to make bread, start bulking up the starter 24 hours ahead of time, adding equal parts bread flour and water every 8 hours.

METRIC CONVERSION CHART

U.S. Measurement	Approximate Metric Liquid Measurement	Approximate Metric Dry Measurement
1 teaspoon	5 ml	–
1 tablespoon or ½ ounce	15 ml	14 g
1 ounce or ⅛ cup	30 ml	29 g
¼ cup or 2 ounces	60 ml	57 g
⅓ cup	80 ml	–
½ cup or 4 ounces	120 ml	113 g
⅔ cup	160 ml	–
¾ cup or 6 ounces	180 ml	–
1 cup or 8 ounces or ½ pint	240 ml	227 g
1½ cups or 12 ounces	350 ml	–
2 cups or 1 pint or 16 ounces	475 ml	454 g
3 cups or 1½ pints	700 ml	–
4 cups or 2 pints or 1 quart	950 ml	–

·➤· ACKNOWLEDGMENTS & SPECIAL THANKS ·➤·

FARMERS & FRIENDS:

Kimball Fruit Farm
Lull Farm
Brookford Farm
Dunk's Mushrooms
Generation Farm
Great Harvest Nashua
New England Fishmongers
Loudonshire Farm
Miles Smith Farm
Rickety Ranch
Field O' Dreams
Steve Normandon Grass-fed Beef
Brookdale Farm
Hillside Apiary
DJ's Pure Natural Honey
Benedikt Dairy
The Robie Farm
Sullivan Farm
Oasis Springs Farm
…and the countless other farms we have worked with
over the last six years. You are the heroes.

A SPECIAL THANKS TO:

Cody Tamaian & Andy Hampton for the amazing pottery and art you create, we are honored to use it.

Deirdre & Aaron of Rusted Pulchritude for the hand-carved spoons and unbelievable work you do.
Thank you so much.

Matthew Lomanno for years of fantastic photography and putting up with us, we love you.

Chef Joe Drift for taking a chance on us and hosting the first ever Farmers Dinner.

Patrick Soucy for being a friend, mentor, and inspiration when I am out of my mind.

Cider Mill Press for the freedom to express our craft.

Thank you to Tiffanie Austin of Aster & Fern for the flower arrangements.

Grant Morris, you believed in us and helped us build media when we couldn't afford it. A million thanks.

Aaron Doherty for believing that this could be a business.

Our staff, who have sacrificed so much to be a part of this vision, we love you all.

Jitti, your friendship and knowledge is a light to everyone who will listen.

Dunk, we are so proud to call you a friend. Thank you for all the knowledge you have given us.

·◆·

PHOTOGRAPHY CREDITS

FOR MY MOTHER

If I have half the kindness in my heart that you did, I will be blessed beyond compare. Your life was a thread woven into every part of me.

May I never unravel.

I love you.

TO MAGGIE,

Rescuing you helped rescue me.

You're a very good dog.

TO JIMMY,

Thank you for believing in me when I didn't believe in myself.

"If a friend isn't doing everything they can to help you succeed, they aren't a friend."

—*K.S.*

CHEF KEITH SARASIN'S love for food was developed at a young age when he would cook for his mother using old cookbooks that were given to him by his grandmother. He began his culinary career at the age of 15, working at a local sub shop washing dishes and making sandwiches. As the years went on he worked his way up through the restaurant ranks, from Sous Chef to Executive Chef. Sarasin was a private chef before founding The Farmers Dinner in 2012.

EMILEE. You are my beacon who gives me hope. My rock who gives me strength. You are one of the most selfless and kindhearted people that I have ever met. The passion you express in all that you do, and the perseverance you have to be the best you can possibly be exemplifies who you are and I appreciate that so much about you. You have been my inspiration and helped me to strive for that same excellence and not to settle for less. Thank you for your patience and unconditional love. And to our pup Oaklee, you have been a blessing. Thank you for the joy you have brought to our lives. I love you both with all my heart!

MY PARENTS YVES AND MYRLENE. Thank you for all that you have done for me. I wouldn't be the man that I am today without you both by my side constantly pushing me to pursue my dreams and achieve my goals. You are my number one fans and with your support I know I can accomplish anything I set my mind to. My older brother Phil, the majority of what I know about photography comes from what I learned from you and I am grateful for that. I look up to you for who you are and all that you have accomplished and I'm so proud of everything that you have set out to do. My younger sisters Kassie and Katie, you are two beautiful young women with extremely bright futures ahead of you and I thank you for always being there when we need you the most. I am truly blessed to have you all in my life and I can't thank you enough. I love you all!

ONE OF MY FIRST MENTORS CHEF JOE MELANSON. If it wasn't for you, I never would have taken the leap to work in Boston, which propelled me to becoming a better chef.

CHEFS CHRIS COOMBS, ADRIENNE WRIGHT, AND STEPHANIE BUI. Thank you for all taking me under your wings fresh out of Johnson & Wales. Without you as my mentors, it would have taken me far longer to get to the point that I am at in my career. I will never forget our time cooking together at The James Beard House and all the times we have shared in between.

TO MY BUSINESS PARTNER KEITH SARASIN. I cannot thank you enough for the opportunity to co-write this cookbook with you. You are filled with so much knowledge and I appreciate your dedication to your craft. We have been able to do such great things together and I have no doubt in my mind that with our future endeavors we can continue to learn and grow together, push each other, and inspire those around us to dream big.

TO MY DAY ONES: JUDE VIAUD, ROBERTO FRANCO, ANTONIO WORMLEY, AND JARED ALLEN. The crazy times and memories that we all share together near and far will never be forgotten. You have in each of your own ways have helped me during some of my toughest times, seen me through many successes, and helped build me up into the person that I am today.

TO ALL OF THE OTHERS who hold a special place in my heart, from family and friends to colleagues and culinary instructors, you all have impacted me greatly in not only my career but the way I carry myself from day-to-day.

—*C.V.*

CHEF CHRIS VIAUD spent three of his most formative years working at Deuxave in Boston, after graduating from Johnson & Wales University in Providence, Rhode Island. He then helped open restaurants in Massachusetts and New Hampshire, using his refined techniques and skill set to advance his career. Today he is the executive chef and co-owner of The Farmers Dinner and Greenleaf in Milford, New Hampshire.

INDEX

∽ ABOUT CIDER MILL PRESS BOOK PUBLISHERS ∾

Good ideas ripen with time. From seed to harvest, Cider Mill Press
brings fine reading, information, and entertainment together between
the covers of its creatively crafted books. Our Cider Mill bears fruit twice
a year, publishing a new crop of titles each spring and fall.

"Where Good Books Are Ready for Press"

Visit us on the Web at
www.cidermillpress.com

or write to us at
PO Box 454
12 Spring St.
Kennebunkport, Maine 04046